Business Continuity for the Public Sector

John Ball AFBCI

Copyright © 2018 John Ball

All rights reserved.

ISBN: 1986149854
ISBN-13: 9781986149853

DEDICATION

I would like to dedicate this book to all who work in the Public Sector. Together, they make the United Kingdom a better, safer place to live.

CONTENTS

	Acknowledgments	i
	About the author	ii
1	Introduction	1
2	Business Continuity Management	6
3	Where to start	16
4	Business Continuity Representatives	29
5	Business Impact Analysis	39
6	The ICT Department	51
7	The BC Plan	58
8	Training and Exercising	76
9	Promoting BC to the organisation	83
10	Continual Improvements	86
11	BC Templates	91
12	Sample Exercise Scenarios	128

ACKNOWLEDGMENTS

Permission to reproduce extracts from ISO 22301 and ISO22313 is granted by BSI. British Standards can be obtained in PDF or hard copy formats from the BSI online shop: **www.bsigroup.com/Shop** or by contacting BSI Customer Services for hardcopies only: Tel: +44 (0)20 8996 9001, Email: **cservices@bsigroup.com**.

Unless otherwise stated, all quotes are from these documents.

Permission to reproduce elements of the joint decision-making model and command structure granted by **www.jesip.org.uk**

For their expertise, and clear eyed attention to detail, in the reviewing and proof reading of this book, I would like to thank:
Julia Connolly MSc. CBCI. ISO22301 lead auditor
Maria Coppard BSc. CBCI.

About the Author

John Ball is a multi-award-winning Business Continuity Manager with over 30 years' experience in the Public Sector. An Associate Fellow of the Business Continuity Institute (BCI), he has a proven track record in BC management and training. He has a wide experience at all levels of response to incidents and emergencies, ranging from helicopter rescue with the Royal Navy Fleet Air Arm at the Fastnet boat race in 1979, to the Shoreham air crash in 2015.

Now working as an independent practitioner, John provides business continuity consultancy, plan exercising and training to the Public Sector.

Awards.
2016 Winner - BCI Global Awards BC in the Public Sector
2016 Winner - BCI European BC Public Sector manager of the year.
2016 Award - Chief Constables Commendation for BC services to Sussex and Surrey Police.
2016 Shortlist - CIR Business Continuity Strategy of the Year
2015 Winner - CIR Public Sector BC Manager of the Year

To contact John or book him for consultancy, training or speaking engagements, email him at **johnball@bcfundamentals.com**

1 INTRODUCTION

The views expressed within this book are my own.

The contents of this book outline my method of approaching Business Continuity (BC) for the Public Sector. It is not the only method, but one that works, and has been recognised by National, European and Global Business Continuity awards.

From the outset I should say that lasting success will only come with a continued application of these processes year on year on year. Business Continuity is not a passing phase like tight trousers or a pie sandwich. It is here to stay, and applied with effort and persistence, will continually improve your organisations ability when responding to, and recovering from a disruption. You have to be in this for the long run.

The Public Sector is not motivated by profit, but by service. With growing demand and diminishing resources, the need to maintain prioritised activities gets more difficult every day. Business Continuity will not provide extra services, but it will keep the services you have got going for longer.

In ancient Greek mythology, the Muses were any of the nine daughters of Zeus and Mnemosyn that symbolised the arts and sciences and gave artists, philosophers and individuals the necessary inspiration for creation.

In the same way, some artists and designers of today often have a particular "muse" in mind when they are working. It helps the creative process and serves as inspiration to produce the best work they can. It may also explain why all the models on the catwalk look the same!

It does not take a great leap of the imagination to see how this idea has been developed into tailoring individual products that are marketed to an identified customer base. But I digress.

I like the idea of a muse and find that utilising this device is quite useful when I am developing and writing BC plans on behalf of organisations and departments. It helps to keep the plan short, simple and relevant to the individual organisation. It doesn't matter if the plan involves manufacturing or service delivery, having the right people in mind when written, will improve its chances of success.

I have two muses that I think about when I am developing BC plans, and they are both anxious people.
The first, is the person that has made contact and needs one of the organisations key services or products.
The second, is the person who works for the organisation and must deliver that key service or product using the Business Continuity plan during a disruption. Which, often, will occur at 2am or Friday afternoon with reduced staff on duty, and the only reference available is the BC plan.
This of course is no bad thing, providing the BC plan is a quality validated product.

I have read some plans that begin with the phrase, "If you are activating this plan, then go to page 57" – this is not ideal and will not inspire confidence in the reader. You can find more information on what I think a good plan looks like in the chapter on BC plans.

Incidentally, if you have to quality assess BC plans, the 2am or Friday afternoon test is a good one to start with.

For me, Business Continuity is simply all about people. In my experience, when BC planning assumptions look after our two muses, the work streams that stem from that will be grounded and relevant. Consequently, resilient services, solid reputation and staff confidence will follow. You may have other muses that you would like to add to this list, but really, if your plan looks after staff and service users, you will be well on the way to developing a resilient organisation that has the ability to bounce back after a disruption.

Planning in this way produces the best return on investment for the organisation as well as creating the following long-term benefits:

- Increased social capital from the workforce
- A loyal customer base
- A reliable and trustworthy reputation
- Confident and capable teams ready to face a disruption
- Customer confidence
- Organisational strength
- Improved layers of resilience

Now that is priceless.

Simply put, the Public Sector is all about people, those who need help and those who deliver it. Business Continuity is all about helping to make that happen.

Everyone within the Public Sector is painfully aware that money is tight across all organisations and buying in Business Continuity skills from the outside can be very expensive, even prohibitive. Yet the requirements of the Civil Contingencies Act 2004 (CCA 2004) remain and must be complied with.

Consequently, it is important to spend the money that is available wisely, and on the right people. This book will show you some creative ideas on how to get best value for your money when introducing, developing and continuing with Business Continuity in your own organisation, and so fulfil the duties set out in the CCA 2004.

The books objectives are to:
- Provide an overview of what is required to develop BC in your organisation.
- Provide an explanatory model of the Business Continuity process that is easy to deliver and understandable by everyone at any level within the organisation.
- Provide a cost-conscious method of delivering Business Continuity management that complies with current cabinet office guidance and aligns with international standards.
- Provide a suitable format for a Business Continuity management system (BCMS) that aligns with international standards and fits in with organisation management practices.

Who should read it.

- **Executive and Senior Managers**. - Will give them an understanding of the leadership commitment and support the BC programme will need if it is to succeed.
- **BC Coordinators / Risk / Resilience/ Emergency Planning Manager**s, (formally trained to BCI certificate level or above) - Will assist in producing a programme of BC development for the organisation that delivers services and keeps the principles of public service at the forefront of planning.
- **Managers and line managers**. Not formally trained. - Will give them sufficient knowledge to understand what the aim of the BC programme is and the support it needs.
- **BC Representatives**. Sufficiently trained to understand the process, but not to certificate level. - Will help them to understand the process of BC and plan writing.
- **Staff**. Not formally trained – will give them an understanding of what BC is and its basic principles.

If you're not on the list but have a responsibility for Business Continuity, then this book is for you as well.
I have set the chapters out in what I think is a logical order, but they are complete within themselves, so can be read in any order that suits you.

Good luck, and I hope you will enjoy the book.

John Ball AFBCI

2 BUSINESS CONTINUITY MANAGEMENT

"The three great essentials to achieve anything worthwhile are; hard work, stick-to-iteveness and common sense" Thomas A Edison.

Origins – Why do we have the CCA 2004?

Prior to the CCA coming into force, the emergency planning arrangements for the UK were principally governed by the Emergency Powers Act 1920, Civil Defence Act 1939, 1948 and Civil protection in Peacetime Act 1986. None of which had been amended in quite some time.

In 2000 and 2001 these acts and provisions were sorely tested in relatively quick succession by the flooding and fuel disputes of 2000 and the foot and mouth outbreak in 2001.

Collectively the country did not cope well. Millions of pounds worth of damage to property, lost revenue to businesses, thousands of lives disrupted and changed, devastation to the rural economy and the destruction of thousands of animals.

In the light of these three events, John Prescott, the deputy prime minister at the time ordered a review into emergency planning and civil protection arrangements in the UK. The review concluded that the current legislation was inadequate, and new legislation was required.

And so, the CCA 2004 was born. Part 1 of the act deals with protective services, community risk, emergency planning and Business Continuity. The Cabinet Office produced the Emergency Preparedness Manual, which gives statutory guidance to part 1 of the act setting out the framework for civil protection in the UK. There are 19 chapters in all, with chapter 6 covering Business Continuity.

The act identifies the emergency services, local authorities and NHS bodies as category 1 responders, and requires them to not only develop plans that maintain protective services during an emergency as far as practicable, but also develop plans that maintain delivery of critical aspects of the day job.

This means that it is ok not to protect everything. A simple enough concept, but I have had some struggles convincing "can do" people of the idea.

Up until this act, most Public Sector organisations did not have any inward facing plans apart from fire drills and evacuation plans, so this is quite a substantial change. The aim of all BC plans is continued service delivery. Business Continuity provides the opportunity to think through your planning in peacetime, which will keep you ahead of the curve – by definition "advanced compared to the rest".

Any kind of incident has the potential to cause a disruption to an organisations operation and its ability to deliver services.

Whilst it is impossible to plan for every eventuality, BC plans should address the most common impacts, people, premises, technology, information, data, specialist equipment and supply chain. I will explore these areas in more detail as we move through the book.

Business Continuity Explained

Business Continuity has been described as common sense written down, which I whole heartedly agree with. In fact, C E Stowe summed up "common sense" in a way which I think describes the process and aims of BC perfectly when he said, *"Common sense is the knack of seeing things as they are and doing things as they ought to be done".* So, adapting his quote I would say that, "BC will help you to see things as they are, and plan to do things as they ought to be done". (Apologies to Mr Stowe.)

Business Continuity is not a dark art shrouded in mystery as many practitioners would have you believe. When you blow away the smoke and mirrors it remains as I have described above, common sense.

There are of course more formal definitions of BC which we will work with. The international standard for BC, ISO 22301, defines Business Continuity as "The capability of the organisation to continue delivery of products or services at acceptable pre-defined levels following a disruptive incident (ISO 22301:2012 3.3).

A useful model.

I would like to share with you an explanation of the Business Continuity management process that I have presented successfully to hundreds of my course delegates. It is a simple model that is quickly understood and makes learning the more detailed principles of the BC process easier.

I have also used this model as an interactive slide show to introduce existing staff and new joiners in the organisation to the idea of Business Continuity, and the organisations commitment to it. It is designed to give staff a basic understanding of the subject without the complicated detail. After all, much of the workforce really only need to know 2 things:

a) That there is a Business Continuity plan for their area of business.

b) What they as individuals must do when it is activated.

Obviously, team leaders, managers and senior managers will understand incrementally more of the process and plan and have differing roles and responsibilities within it. However, I have found that this little model, as they say in the quiz programme, is a very good starter for 10, so here it is.

Imagine that you work for yourself, and without work you have no income.

Now, from the list of activities below, choose one that will have the biggest impact on you if you **stopped** doing it.

- Decorating the house
- Gardening
- Going to work by car
- Hobbies
- Holidays

Clearly, stopping going to work will have the biggest impact, as we have already established that without work there is no income generated.

Consequently, having identified the most important activity from the list, we must work out how to protect it. It can also be said that under these circumstances going to work by car can be considered a time critical activity.

Before you can drive your car, there is certain legislation that you will have to comply with, you will require:

- Tax
- Insurance
- Driving Licence for that type of vehicle
- MOT (if required)

Supply Chain. There is a supply chain attached to this activity as your vehicle will require fuel, water, tyres and oil. Most people have a favourite garage they go to for these supplies, and even a secondary one if it is closed.

At this point, you could now drive in and out of work – **BUT,** there are risks.

Risk Assessment. This activity needs a risk assessment, as cars can:

- Breakdown
- Be stolen
- Be involved in a collision
- Get a puncture

Because these risks pose a threat to our main activity, we must think of a way to reduce them where we can. It may not be possible to reduce all the risks because of cost or the remote likelihood of them happening. However, in this case, putting some simple measures in place will be very effective.

Risk Reduction. Risk reduction for our current risks could be as follows:

- Regular car maintenance
- Fit a car alarm
- Spare Tyre
- Join a recovery service

Though these measures will significantly reduce the risks to our activity, because of its importance we should go a stage further. If all the risk reduction fails, you will still have to get into work, so an alternative method of getting there is required, and will in effect form a BC plan.

Options for alternative transport to work.

- Public transport
- Lift / walk / bicycle
- Replacement vehicle

Apart from a replacement vehicle, the remaining alternatives, though less efficient and take more time, ensure that the activity of getting to work can be completed.

The principles we have just applied to our home activities and car journey, are scalable, and can be applied in the same way to the activities of an organisation or the departments within it. They can be summarised as follows:

Summary
- From a list of activities select those most time critical
- Understand any legal requirements
- Understand any associated supply chain
- Risk assess the activity – what can go wrong
- Mitigate / reduce the risk where possible
- Work out a way to continue with the activity – though at a reduced level = BC PLAN.

Remember this model is designed to give a basic understanding of how Business Continuity works to a complete novice and will be fine for the average worker. Obviously, those who have a greater responsibility for the BC process will require more expertise and detail, which follows in the book.

Available guidance.

ISO 22301/ 22313 – Requirements / Guidance.
The international standard for Business Continuity ISO 22301 / 22313 – Requirements / Guidance is the most commonly used standards within the Public Sector and elsewhere. It replaced BS25999, the British standard for BC in 2012, and is currently under review. Available from the BSI group for just over £200.00 to non-members.

It is possible to get certificated as compliant with this standard at a cost, and a few Public Sector organisations have done just that. However, in my experience, a clear majority see no cost benefit in compliance, but they do seek to align to it as suggested by the Cabinet Office.

By aligning to the standard, your BC programme will have guidance, direction and credibility as you work through it. Also, when it comes to auditing your organisation for BC, the standard is where the auditors will look to set their inspection strategy.

Remember, slavish adherence to this standard will not produce a magic set of BC plans that will work perfectly. Use them to guide you through the process, **but** the result must fit your organisation and the way that you work. Don't make following the process the thing, make it part of the thing – if that makes sense.

ISO/TS 22317 – Guidance for Business Impact Analysis.

This technical specification for the completion of a Business Impact Analysis (BIA) was published in 2015. This is a logical enough document, but to the irritation of some BC professionals it missed out the risk assessment part of the process. Available from the BSI group for around £100.00.

Emergency Preparedness Manual.

The emergency preparedness manual is the cabinet office guidance to the CCA 2004 and is freely available on line. It sets out a generic framework for civil protection with duties for category 1 and 2 responders. It contains 19 chapters and several annexes. Some chapters worthy of note are Integrated Emergency Management in chapter 1, Emergency Planning chapter 5, Business Continuity chapter 6, Business Continuity advice – duty for local authorities' chapter 8, chapter 9 for London, chapter 10 for Scotland, chapter 11 for Wales and chapter 12 for Northern Ireland.

Chapter 6 makes several references to BS25999, the old standard for Business Continuity, which is no longer in use. Though no longer in use, the principles they espouse are sound.

Expectations and Indicators of Good Practice Set for Cat 1 and 2 Responders.

This is a Cabinet Office document revised in October 2013, and freely available from their website. This document aims to clarify what is expected of category 1 and 2 responders in England and Wales in relation to:

- Their duties set out in CCA 2004
- Contingency Planning Regs 2005
- National Resilience Capabilities Programme
- Emergency Response and Recovery

Essentially this is what the Cabinet Office thinks "good" looks like – well worth a read.

Business Continuity Institute (BCI) Good Practice Guidelines 2018.

The BCI good practice guidelines are a world-wide, industry acknowledged set of guidelines for producing and developing Business Continuity within an organisation. They provide a framework to structure the approach to Business Continuity.

I have been using these guidelines for years and find them to be a useful addition full of promising ideas on how to develop BC. Well worth keeping in the toolbox. Available on the BCI website £20.00

Business Continuity for Dummies.

The clue is in the title, this book was sponsored by the Cabinet Office, Business Continuity Institute and the Emergency Planning Society. I think it's a good book, but definitely not for dummies. I don't think many newcomers would get far using this book without additional training.

Business Continuity for the Public Sector – Right people, right place, right time. By John Ball

An excellent book on how to introduce BC to the Public Sector. Practical and full of useful information revealing the simple side of the dark arts. (sorry, couldn't resist.)

3 WHERE TO START

"Being open minded isn't the same as having a hole in the head".
Peter Walker.

The Executive Team – the will and scope
The will.

It doesn't really matter whether you are just starting with BC or refreshing the old programme for either a business unit or the entire organisation, your efforts will go nowhere until and unless you have active meaningful engagement from the top management. This is an old mantra and trotted out by every professional who ever speaks or writes on the subject. It is however a fundamental truth.

Active and meaningful engagement is much more than a nod from the boss and a "yes we will have Business Continuity, let me know when it's done" approach.

I have operated under this kind of agreement before, and I can tell you it's rubbish. The organisation will roll its eyes when you mention BC, and take a long time doing nothing, because without top cover it's a waste of time.

ISO 22301 has included a section on leadership and management commitment to the Business Continuity Management System and includes the provision and allocation of resources to get the job done.

This section also speaks of a commitment to absorb Business Continuity requirements into the organisations business processes.

When you have this kind of commitment from the top team, I can tell you it is a joy to go to work.

I worked under these conditions for Sussex Police with Giles York QPM as Chief Constable, and Olivia Pinkney QPM, currently the Chief Constable of Hampshire.

Both were actively involved and interested in the development of BC within the service, and clearly saw the contribution that Business Continuity made to organisation resilience. Because of this level of support, Sussex Police, developed one of the best Business Continuity management systems in the country.

Scope.

The next piece of information you will need executive team to sign off on, is the scope of the Business Continuity programme, what's in, what's out. This strategic view is important, because it will help the rest of the organisation to see where their unit or department supports the key objectives, and therefore, which parts of the business will need a plan.

I cannot overemphasise the importance of this document, it provides an excellent focus for everyone concerned. It also makes it much easier for BC coordinators and Representatives to explain to colleagues why they need to produce a plan.

The Collins English Dictionary defines core business as "the activity that is the main source of a company's profits and success, usually the activity that the company was set up to carry out". If you are a Public Sector organisation, then for "profits" read "services".

This should be a top line assessment by the executive and consist of those activities that are fundamental to the organisations existence. Not a list of long term intentions or aspirations, but the real time core business activities that you do not want to stop doing.

Once set, the entire organisation will be able to see how and to what degree individual departments support core business activities. It will also help in deciding criticality during the business impact analysis process, giving implied permission to set aside those things that are not so critical during a disruption.

In addition, these top line activities can form the basis of a strategic level plan for the senior management team during the response and recovery phase of an event. All in all, a very useful list to have thought through.

I had imagined that most organisation would have done this work already, but after a fair amount of research across company and Public Sector web sites, with but two exceptions, I could not find any reference to core business activities. I found many references to productivity, strategic objectives, ethics, mission statements, diversity, aims, values, employee retention, core values, customer service and principles.

Some of these headings sounded promising, and all necessary, but none had the kind of information I was looking for. It may be of course that this work has been done but is not published, however going by some of the BC policies I have seen lately, my guess is, it remains on the "to do" list.

Here are some of the benefits that articulating the core business activities of an organisation will bring:

- A clear statement from the executive team about what is important.
- Clarity for the workforce – answers the "what we are about" question.

- Clarity for BC planners – they know exactly what needs protection and where to focus initial effort and resource.
- Clarity for investors, service users and customers – they all know what to expect from the organisation.
- An initial strategic plan for the executive team during the response and recovery phases of a disruption, or as the basis of a plan for an event picked up on horizon scanning.
- A baseline around which creative management can work when dealing with the unexpected.

If you ask most executive officers of a Public Sector organisation what are the six most important things that they would not want to stop doing, they will have a pretty good idea, and could probably write you a list there and then.

There is a school of thought that believes this method is the only way of getting this information and go no further than that in the creation of their core business activities. However, I prefer a methodology with a little more evidential substance.

I have also found that presenting the top team with an evidence-based list of core business for them to consider, also gives them the opportunity to add non-evidence-based activities if they so wish.

If the organisation you work for is a Police force, these core activities can be distilled from the Crime Commissioners Police and Crime Plan, the Chief Constables policing plan and the government key policing targets. In addition to the core business activities, here are some other factors that may be relevant and so can be considered when determining scope:

- Legal or regulatory requirement
- Perceived high risk location
- Income streams. e.g. parking revenue, road safety speed cameras, commercial property rentals.
- Customer requirement

"We will answer and respond to emergency calls" is an example of a core business activity you might come up with from those documents.

Now, think about how many departments there are within the service that directly support that single activity. Here are a few:

- Call centre
- IT department
- Estates
- Patrol officers
- Police vehicles
- Finance

Of the many varied activities that each of these departments will carry out on a daily basis, the ones that support the strategic objective will be the activities they will aim to preserve during a disruption.

I have recently completed some work with a local authority on their Business Continuity programme, and we were able to form a strategic list of core business activities from their corporate plan, strategic risk register and operational risk register. This list now informs the production and development of Business Continuity plans across all areas of work.

In every case the strategic elements of the scope should be signed off by the executive group before the detailed work of BC begins. The strategic list of core business is an important piece to get right, because it will become the keystone that holds the rest of the programme together.

Circumstances that will affect the scope, such as reorganisation, can of course change the look and objectives of the organisation, which will mean that the scope will have to change with it.

In recent years, the Public Sector has been in a state of constant change and reordering, brought about by cuts and the idea that you can do more for less. Because this has left very little margin for error in the operating capability of service providers, I think that Business Continuity is needed more now than ever.

All in all, a simple, strategic list of core business activities is a beautiful thing, and certainly worth developing if you don't have one.

Business Continuity Policy

Having guided the core business activities through the Executive Board, the next logical step, certainly within the Public Sector is to create the Policy. The Policy is the foundation of the entire BC programme, and contains the organisations declaration of intent as to how BC will be dealt with and who will be responsible for it.

A Business Continuity Policy (BC) is like a mirror. When you look into it, it should reflect, as sect 3.38 of ISO22301 puts it – "the intentions and direction of an organisation as formally expressed by its top management."

A Policy provides the framework for the development of BC within an organisation based on its aspirations and objectives.

It should not leave the reader in any doubt as to what the organisations position is on BC, who is responsible for it and how to go about complying with it. If it doesn't do that, then not only will the reader be lost and not know what is expected of them, but an early opportunity to promote Business Continuity has also been lost.

This week, look at your organisations Policy and see what it looks like.

- Does it reflect the intentions and directions formally expressed by top management?
- Is your organisation doing what the Policy says it will do regarding its BC Programme?
- Is what is happening out in the workplace the same as what the Policy says should be happening?

The Policy is the life force that gives BC credence within an organisation, and so I think is worth spending time on, to get it right.

I have added a specimen Policy in the "templates" chapter that I think aligns well with the ISO guidance and would be suitable for public or Private Sector. In addition, the appendices that are mentioned in the Policy have been added as separate templates, which you may or may not want to use.

Who is going to do it?

In the early years of CCA 2004 many Public Sector organisations took the advice suggested in the emergency preparedness manual and appointed a specific person to the role of BC Manager or Coordinator.

Trained to a recognised standard, usually the BCI Certificate, this person then became responsible for implementing Business Continuity across the whole organisation. No easy task, when you consider how receptive most organisations are to changing things they are familiar with, let alone something completely new.

Things have moved on a pace since then, and in many cases I find that BC management, Emergency Planning and Risk Management are dealt with by one person under the title of "Resilience Manager ". Personally, I think that merging different skill sets into one is not ideal, however I understand that organisations must "cut their cloth" according to the pressures they face.

This, in some cases, as before, leaves a single person responsible for the content and writing of all of the organisation BC plans. Whilst this approach may work on a few control levels, I think it is flawed, because it does not involve the rest of the organisation in Business Continuity to any depth.

Assisting departments to write their own plan will improve plan quality because they know their part of the business better than anyone else. It also gives them responsibility and ownership of their activities and how they maintain them.

I have found that having a BC Coordinator leading several BC Representatives is a very effective way of implementing, developing plans and embedding Business Continuity within the organisation without a specific budget.

The BC Coordinator / Manger will have to be trained to a higher level to be able to assist everyone else, so there will be a cost there, but the return on investment is good.

Useful Tip. It is worth noting that apart from the nominated expert, everyone else in the organisation that takes on Business Continuity responsibilities, will almost certainly be carrying them out in addition to their day job. And because of that, you the practitioner will find that BC goes to the very bottom of everyone's list. So, despite having top level authority you will need all your charm, sensitivity, and cunning to get the job done.

Change – who moved my cheese?

Part of developing a trouble-free life at work, is learning to embrace change. Now, despite what I hear the zealots of change say about how great and empowering change is, I'm not convinced they really mean it. I would go further to say that privately, absolutely no one likes to change at all.

However, it is a fact of life and we do have to learn to cope with it. If you must introduce any change or deal with changes yourself, I would recommend you read a short book by Dr Spenser Johnson entitled "Who Moved my Cheese" – brilliant. I worked on a department once that was facing major change, and we were all sent a copy to read, to help us cope.

I have also come up with my own method of dealing with change, which works well for me and I would like to share with you.

It consists of four letters: A, A, A and S. Here is what they stand for:

- **A**ccept the change, its coming.
- **A**dapt to the change, get the best from it.
- **A**dvance with the change, that's how things are being done now.
- **S**ulk, sulking is ok, even healthy, **but**, sulking is only allowed up to the Advance stage, and not at all after.

There are no set time periods for each phase, but the trick is to remember to apply the process in time.

Big bang or organic?

When I had my first go at introducing BC into an organisation in 2007, my old boss at the time decided we would go for the big bang approach.

The BC Representatives were nominated, and would all be given the information at the same time on how to complete a business impact analysis (BIA), how to fill out the plan templates and a deadline to finish the work by.

The theory being that at the end of the deadline we would have all the plans that we needed, and that would be that – job done.

How wrong can you be – I laugh about it now, but this single act had the effect of turning off the entire workforce to business continuity, and in some cases generating some high-powered animosity.

So then, not only did we still have a tricky subject to introduce, and get some plans written, we had to do it with an alienated workforce.

The programme did not have a specific budget, so any money we needed had to be found from existing cashflow. I got quite good at it in the end, and never had a problem with money for BC after that period.

Useful Tip. In hindsight, the big bang approach may have gone better if we had:

- Trained the BC Coordinator to a higher level.
- Trained the BC Representatives to a fundamental level of knowledge of BC
- Spent more time introducing the idea to the organisation to reduce obstacles
- Developed simpler templates
- Better understood the workload that we were generating for already busy people

Because we didn't train the BC Representatives well enough, the plans that did come back where not consistent in quality, and far too lengthy. We had plenty of plans, but I was not convinced of their efficacy should we face a disruption. We needed to do better.

Organic

BC is not a one-off activity, it is ever moving ever changing and needs constant attention by the coordinator if it is to remain an effective tool for the organisation.

The decision was made to re-introduce the BC programme into the organisation, but at a slower pace, with the aim of improving both the quality of the product and the reputation of the discipline, which had suffered since the big bang approach.

The problem is selecting a starting point. A good resolution to this is to select a key department that would be keen to have you work with their BC representative and help them to complete their plan.

The obvious candidates will be evident from the list of core business activities, and will likely consist of theICT department, Contact Centre, or one of your front-line service providers. So, I would suggest you start there.

Busy departments will be delighted at this offer of assistance and through it you will make many new friends, which at the initial stages of this process will help a lot.

You will find this process is slower, but the outcomes are better and will help to control plan quality, as well as providing on the job learning for the BC Representatives that you work with.

Over time, word will get around, your phone will start to ring, and other departments will be keen to know when it will be their turn, and so slowly the organisation wakes up to BC everywhere.

This phased approach worked very well for me, and I would recommend it as a way of introducing BC into the organisation for the first time, or as an iterative programme year on year.

Bench mark / Gap analysis – where are you now?

Benchmarking where you are now with regard to the state of BC within the organisation is important at the start of your programme. It will help you to develop work streams, build reports and demonstrate progress to senior management.

If BC is new to your organisation, then it's easy, you're starting at the bottom. If you are revisiting or renewing the process, then you will probably need to produce a "gap analysis". This will inform you how much work needs to be done to move the organisation from where you are now to where you want to be.

A simple but effective way of doing this is by creating an ISO22301 audit tool in the form of a spread sheet based on the standard. You will find this useful as most organisations want to align with the standard rather than take the expensive certificate route.

The tool will highlight the areas of work that have been completed or in place, and those that have yet to be done – so quite a simple but effective gap analysis.

During the first three years of the above mentioned programme I arranged an annual survey of all staff with some simple questions designed to show at what level the knowledge of BC was filtering through to the organisation.

Not surprisingly, the executive team and senior managers were the first to acknowledge BC, followed by middle managers, line managers, team leaders and staff.

Useful Tip. The level of knowledge and detail that each of these groups needs to understand is different, and so expect at least three years before you can statistically demonstrate organisation wide understanding to the top team.

Eventually, as your BC programme gains maturity, and becomes part of the way you do business, the question of performance statistics and key performance indicators will eventually be raised. I will cover this in more detail in the chapter on continuous improvements

4 BUSINESS CONTINUITY REPRESENTATIVES (BC REP)

"It is amazing what you can get done when you don't mind who gets the credit". Harry S Truman.

Who should they be?

As I have already mentioned, a lot of people within the Public Sector are doing more than one job already, so getting volunteers will not be easy, in fact some may have to be nominated by management.

Most Police forces are divided up into territorial areas of operations with their own command group that is responsible for that specific area. Often each of these areas will have an operational planning team that are responsible for planning the policing for events such as marches and football.

Many of these planning teams will also include an area Emergency Planning Officer in their number. Even though BC is a Risk Management process, I think it is more closely related to the operational and Emergency Planning team. And because of their planning skills, I would suggest that this group would be the best place to recruit a BC Representative.

There are staff with these types of skills across the rest of the Public Sector, health, local authorities, fire and rescue. Though I find that the numbers of people are dwindling, leaving a larger area of operations for those that remain.

In the case of smaller Local Authorities, with two to three hundred staff, it is likely that there won't be anyone with the skills required to take on the role of BC Representative, so they must come from somewhere else within the business.

The last Local Authority I worked for solved this problem by passing the task on to their service managers to complete.

I provided the relevant training for this group in the form of a series of workshops over a number of weeks, which worked very well.

We also held several one-day business continuity surgeries throughout the period to deal with any problems that had arisen as they applied the training to their areas of work. If you would like to know more about this kind of workshop, Contact me via **johnball@bcfundamentals.com**

What type of training do they require?

BC Representatives who are given the BC plan to develop or update should as a matter of course be given some formal training to assist them.

Within my former organisation, Surrey and Sussex Police, this training took the form of either a two-day BC fundamentals course or development course, delivered by an outside trainer. This was very successful and properly equipped staff, (with some guidance from me) to produce BC plans for their area of work.

Our approach worked well for the first year, but because of staff turnover across the service, we found that the following year we needed to repeat the process. Again, no bad thing, because those that had moved on within the organisation, took with them a basic knowledge of BC.

At year three, we decided that the training was still necessary, but the outside training costs had become prohibitive. To solve this problem, I put a cost savings measure to senior management, which they agreed to, and as a result, I attended night school for three months to attain a City and Guilds in Education and Training.

Being now qualified to train adults, I was able to deliver annually a BC fundamentals and plan development course that I had written, to staff across both forces.

This approach saved an average of £10k per year on outside training costs, allowed us to train our own people regularly, and in addition, provide training to Local Resilience Forum partners at the same time.

Senior and middle managers that attended this course found that it improved their knowledge and understanding of BC, which in turn enabled them to give the correct level of support to staff that are tasked with developing their plan.

The costs to the organisation associated with this course are minimal and break down as follows; in house training venue, "on costs", staff salary, two days away from the day job and the price of two BC text books given to each delegate.

I think that the best time to deliver training of this kind, particularly if you need a working budget to buy books for example, is between January and March. I have found over the years that almost all departments have money that they are looking to spend before the end of the financial year, or face losing it from the following year's budget.

I can already hear finance shouting "it's not like that anymore", well, my experience is that either departmentally or collectively across the organisation, there is very often some money available at this time of year. By charging departments as little as £120 per head from their end of year surplus, I was able to provide an excellent course for their BC Representatives, and was able to underwrite those Representatives from less fortunate departments so that they could also attend the course.

Using this format for training staff, resulted in a low-cost Business Continuity continual improvement model that proved successful in providing:

- An affordable annual business continuity training for staff at all levels.
- Significant cost savings on outside training.
- Staff trained to a consistent standard.
- Widespread promotion of the organisations core values and objectives.
- Continuous improvement and embedding of BC awareness within the organisation.
- Identification of home grown future experts in BC who understand the organisation and how it works.
- A capability that can boost production or service delivery at little or no cost.
- Continuous growth in organisation resilience.
- Robust BC plans.

Standing up in front of a group of people and training them is not for everyone, but if you can do it, I can thoroughly recommend it as a way of delivering quality BC training to your organisation and save money at the same time. The City and Guilds introduction to Education and Training, is available at most colleges at a cost of around £400.00 and is all that you will need to be able to train adults. The return on investment is as I have pointed out above, excellent.

Useful Tip. Whether you buy in a trainer or do it yourself It is important to get an "A" lister to open your BC course. Only the chief officer, chief executive or one of their deputies will do. This sends a strong message to the course delegates about the organisations commitment to the programme, and sets the right tone.

Useful Tip. Executive officers time is at a premium, so it is important to book them early. However it is also very handy to get them to make a video introducing BC and opening the course. You can use this if they cant make it. It is much better to have them present, but the video is a good standby, and a very close second.

Useful Tip. Which ever method you decide to use, only tell the course delegates that the chief executive will be opening the course. This will guarantee that every one will be early on day one, and ready to go.

A word about BC rep's

It is important to remember and be sensitive to the fact, that the role of BC rep will be an additional task for already busy people, and as such will easily drop to the bottom of their "to do" list very easily, so tread softly.

Because initially, this is a big piece of work, even after some training it is worth taking time to reassure your Reps that:

- They will receive appropriate training to complete the task.
- They will be supported throughout the process.
- The executive team have committed themselves to providing the resources and time to complete what is being asked of them.
- The role becomes easier after the first phase is completed.

You may also from time to time, have to remind your BC Reps managers that the executive team has committed the organisation to this process they should allow them time to do it.

What is the BC Rep's role?

If your organisation is introducing Business Continuity for the first time, your BC Reps will be taking on quite a big piece of work in the first phase of the programme. It may be a little less daunting if you are refreshing or re-establishing the BC programme, as some may have heard of the subject before, but even so, it will be a busy time. The second phase of the role is a little less busy and can be considered as the maintenance phase of the programme.

Phase 1

Training

The first phase generally will consist of training the BC Representatives up to an acceptable standard. Now this does not mean that you must pay out thousands of pounds for them all to take the BCI certificate.

If you are doing the training yourself you can keep costs to a minimum, control the quality and content of the message and keep the training focused on the way that your organisation works.

By this time, you should have your core business activities in place, and so be able to introduce them to your Reps during the training. This is particularly useful, as it allows the Reps see the relevance of their departmental activities within the organisations structure.

If you are not delivering the training yourself, you can provide BC fundamentals training by using an outside trainer, as we did in the initial stages of our programme. If you do take this route, try to find a consultant who will work with you and tailor the training to suit your organisation, rather than just bringing along a bog-standard fundamentals package.

Business Impact Analysis (BIA)

Once trained, and early task for your BC Representatives will be to complete a business impact analysis (BIA) for their respective area of the business. See Chapter 5 below.

This is not a simple task, and so they will need your regular help and guidance through the process to achieve the results you're looking for. You will find a step by step guide on how to complete a BIA along with relevant forms in the Templates chapter.

This is not the only way to conduct a BIA, but a way that has worked for me, and one that newcomers to business continuity tell me is easy to use.

The Plan

Now for the easy bit. After all this detailed work, the actual Business Continuity Plan can be written, and if the preceding work has been done carefully, writing the plan, really is the simplest part. I have included my version of a BC Plan, in the Templates chapter of this book which you may find useful.

Just a word on what I think about plans. The Oxford English Dictionary describes the definition of a plan as follows: *"a plan is a detailed proposal for doing or achieving something, an intention or decision about what one is going to do".*

This is exactly what I think a Business Continuity plan ought to seek to achieve. It should not be a list of promising ideas or intentions, but a list of actions. A plan should take you somewhere, and quickly. I will cover plan strategy and implementation in more detail in the chapter on BC plans.

Phase 2

In phase 2, the BC Rep's role becomes a little less busy in the second phase of the programme and will eventually settle down into the maintenance and running of the BC plan and its associated duties.

Validation

For the new plan to be of any use at all it will have to be seen by the people that it affects, signed off by department management and validated by being subjected to an exercise.

Useful Tip. I would not dive into planning an exercise immediately but would take time to let colleagues affected by the plan, have a look at it. Very often they will have innovative ideas that can be incorporated into the plan structure at an early stage.

In my experience, the more exposure that people have to a plan that affects them, the more committed they will be to it and making it work.

I will be dealing with plan exercising in more detail later in the chapter on Training and Exercising. There will also be several scenario suggestions for you to use in   Chapter 12.

Risks

In the application of the BC process the Reps will identify risks, that in some cases the organisation will not be aware that it faces. How this risk is dealt with will depend on the risk appetite of the organisation and its relationship is with Risk Management and Business Continuity. Usually departments will be expected to deal with a certain level of risk locally but will have to escalate some risks for a business decision to be made.

The BC rep will form part of the risk identification and reporting process which should fit into the risk management structure for the organisation. I have added a common structure for governance in the body of the specimen BC Policy and its Appendix B in the chapter on templates.

The BC Group

Do not lose contact with the Reps once this piece of work has been completed, because Business Continuity is an ongoing activity and will require both yours and their constant attention.

The BC Reps should form a BC Group, that will cover the whole organisation. They are the eyes and ears of the BC coordinator, and are also the means by which the BC directions of the executive body can be carried out.

I found that meeting with this group four times per year was sufficient to deal with the work that had to be done, though some organisations meet more regularly.

I have added a specimen Terms of Reference (TOR) paper for this meeting cycle in the templates chapter.

5 BUSINESS IMPACT ANALYSIS (BIA)

"The process of analysing activities and the effect that a business disruption might have on them". (ISO 22301,2012 3.8)

About the BIA

Conducting a BIA is probably the most interesting, thought provoking and fascinating process that you can be involved in whilst being paid. BIAs are amazing and will reveal to you in great detail exactly how everything works within the department or organisation you are dealing with and also highlight both its strengths and weaknesses.

It is very easy to get bogged down with this process, to over think it and make it much more complicated than it really is. Try to avoid paralysis by analysis, it is both time consuming and distracting.

Essentially what you're aiming to do is find out which of your organisations activities are the most important, and by planning, prevent them from going under during a disruption. The summary from the car analogy in chapter 1 puts it simply:

- From a list of department or organisation activities, select those most time critical
- Understand any legal requirements
- Understand any associated supply chain
- Risk assess the activity – what can go wrong
- Mitigate / reduce the risk where possible

Work out a way to continue with the activity – though at a reduced level = BC PLAN

When to do one

After the BC Policy has been agreed and put in place, the core business activities have been established and the business continuity Representatives have been nominated and trained, the time will be right to start on the BIA trail. This is a daunting prospect, and best approached as I mentioned in the "organic" phase of Chapter 2, one department at a time.

BIA Methodology

The BIA method will help to isolate the time critical / prioritised activities for each area of the business, after which the more detailed work can begin on finding out how each activity is delivered. When considering what impact criteria to use against time on your activities, I would concentrate on the "operational" effect of not providing services.

Because you're in the Public Sector, stopping any key service will automatically influence "reputation", with negative perceptions likely to escalate at the same rate as the operational impact, so concentrating on the one element will produce most of the information you will need to separate out your time critical/ prioritised activities.

It is always possible to refine the impacts further using financial, reputational and location criteria after the list has been shortened to a more manageable group.

There are several ways of getting at the information that you need, and the methods that you choose will depend on the type of organisation you're part of. I used a combination of spreadsheet questionnaires and interviews. By far the best of these is the interview, you get much more information from a wide-ranging discussion. However, used in the right way, the spreadsheet questionnaires can be very effective.

Be careful with spreadsheets, and especially how you display the information within them. When I tried to collect the BIA information the first time, my spreadsheet had several different tabs that were configured to eventually hold all the critical information from the departments BIA, set out in a logical order.

Logical to me of course, because I wrote it.

However, what I did not expect, was the overwhelming affect that seeing all this information had on the candidates. Many felt the task was too great, and they were too busy to deal with it all. This was despite sending out careful instructions as to the bit that I did want them to complete.

Useful Tip. The next time I sent the spreadsheet out, I hid the other tabs electronically, so that the only worksheet visible to the candidates was the page that I wanted them to complete. It was a bit like putting blinkers on a horse, but worth it, as it is prevented any further angst from the candidates and allowed me to get the work done a bit at a time.

I also like spreadsheets because it's easy to store individual departmental BC information on them, and the data can easily be compared with other information you are collecting across other departments.

I would suggest that when you are conducting a BIA for any department or smaller unit, that you **take time out** as soon as you have:

- established a list of their activities
- And from that list, have identified those activities that have the greatest impact to the business when lost. These will become your time critical/prioritised activities.

The reason for stopping at this stage is to show the list to the departmental management. At this point, management may well decide to add to the list a critical/prioritised activity that has not been identified by analysis or even remove activities they think do not belong to them.

When I carried this process out for one department and showed them to the management, they were surprised to find that some of the activities identified where not part of their role at all. Consequently, these activities were stopped, passed on to their rightful owner and at a stroke, released staff from doing things that were not their responsibility, thereby freeing up a bit of time.

Useful Tip. If you have collected spreadsheet information from several individuals within a department, it is worth anonymising the results before you show them to management.

Not everyone will have the same view on what is important and what has the greatest impact, and so one or two statistical outliers will be generated. A statistical outlier is a result that is remotely and hugely different from the rest of the data and can be discounted.

By collecting the knowledge of the many and ignoring the outliers, you will get a very accurate picture of what the team thinks the impacts of loss over time are.

Once management have agreed that the list is accurate, only then should the more detailed work begin.

Suppliers External and Internal

External

Most large organisations will have hundreds, and in some cases thousands of contracts with outside suppliers, that provide services and goods to the organisation, ranging from printer ink to vehicles. It is both pointless and impractical to consider the business continuity arrangements of every supplier to the organisation. There is simply no need.

What I would suggest though, is to consider the BC arrangements of those suppliers that provide goods or services to your time critical/prioritised activities, which you will find narrows the list considerably.

A good deal of this work can be done via the procurement department, although do not be surprised if they are unable to tell you which of their supplier's, service time critical/prioritised activities.

Useful Tip. Getting the procurement department to add conditions about business continuity as a standard feature of their contract bidding/tendering process is a must, and the sooner it's done the better. This will mean that companies bidding for a contract with the organisation will not qualify to the final stages of the process unless they can produce a BC plan. Again, not practical for the smaller contracts, but a must for the larger ones.

This also means that if you are the BC Coordinator, you can ask to see it.

Be wary of outsourcing companies, those who will win the contract but outsource the work to smaller, less resilient businesses.

A recent example of the danger of this is the fall of the building contractor Carrillion. Over exposure to a single supplier without having a plan should they fail has left many government projects suspended, with the associated loss of jobs and business failures. It would be interesting to see just what their BC plan looked like, that is assuming they had one.

Useful Tip. If you're an organisation that operates a large fleet of vehicles, such as ambulance, fire and rescue or Police, check out your bulk fuel arrangements. Who is your supplier, how much bunkered stock do you keep, how long will that last, and finally how much fuel will the supplier guarantee to deliver to you, when they face a disruption. The answers to these questions may be encouraging or frightening. You won't know until you ask.

Useful Tip. If your organisation does operate a large fleet and uses fuel cards so that fuel can be obtained either from your own sources or commercial outlets, make sure that the expiry dates for these cards are staggered. I am aware of one large company where 50% of their fuel cards expired on the same day. Easily done, but best avoided.

Useful Tip. If you have a current supplier that you like and works well with you, and they don't have a BC plan, give them advice on how to get one.

Useful Tip. If you are a local authority and are buying commercial property for income generation, make sure you have a BC plan to service any loans should the property bubble burst. Over exposure to a single market can be risky, so needs a plan.

Internal

As you collect more detailed information in the BIA, there is no doubt that for the majority of departments, the Information and Communications Technology (ICT) department will turn out to be a major internal supplier. An obvious statement, one might think. However, you will be surprised at just how different the ICT department priorities can differ from those of the organisation. This is where the information from the BIA can help.

Useful Tip. Once completed, collect all of the systems information from your organisations BC plans and tell the ICT department what they are. These systems are essentially what keeps the business running, and whilst ICT will have a good idea about the obvious ones such as Outlook, telephony and communications, they may be in the dark about the rest. With this additional information, they are able to re prioritise their efforts, and occasionally budget, to make sure the right systems are recovered first after a failure.

The BIA report

When the work on individual BIAs is completed, I have found it useful to produce a report on the findings of the BIA for senior management. This report outlines what has been found, any single points of failure and any mitigations of risk that may be possible at an early stage.

The report helps management to understand the scope of what is required, to assess what has been discovered against the organisation risk appetite and to sign off on any actions that have been suggested.

I have produced a short fictional example of a report below to demonstrate what I mean.

Speed Detection Department (SDD) – Business Impact Analysis (BIA)

Information

This BIA relates to the SDD, and associated departments that are concerned with the collection, recording and processing of speeding offences detected by speed cameras. The purpose of the information in this document is to expose potential risk and allow appropriate Business Continuity solutions to be selected that will maintain key activities during a disruption.

The information directly relates to the delivery of three, time critical activities whose minimum levels of service are:

1. Visit xx mobile camera site visits per day.
2. Visit xx wet film cameras send film for processing every 8 days
3. Daily download of camera data from xx digital cameras

Where concentrated areas of risk are identified they will be described as Single Points of Failure (SPOF) and will be accompanied by suggested mitigation.

There are three principal areas of business that support speed detection by camera; The Camera Team & Cameras, Film Processing and administration Department.

The process has been broken down into its constituent parts and will be dealt with individually within the report to provide an understanding of how each element works.

Camera Team and Cameras

The camera team consist of xx Supervisor/s and xx Camera Technicians based at Anytown unit base, all of which are trained to the same skill level. The team have access to a number of Mercedes vans and a single Peugeot van with which to carry out their duties.

The speed data is gathered by three types of camera:
- Wet Film Speed — xxx fixed units
- Wet Film Red Light - xxx fixed units
- Digital Speed - xxx fixed units
- Mobile Speed- xxx mobile units

Daily — Each of the mobile cameras are calibrated using fixed markings in the garage area at the Anytown location. These calibrations have been drawn and set up by a specialist team, the measurements of which are supported by statement.

Daily — The digital camera data is accessed via a standalone computer at the Anytown base by a member of the camera team, and the data is downloaded to a disc, which is the primary evidence disc. This disc is then uploaded to a drive via a networked computer at Anytown base. The disc is then stored at Anytown.

Daily - Each member of the camera team is expected to visit up to xx mobile camera sites using the equipment in the mobile units. The mobile camera equipment creates a disc, which is copied and uploaded to drive via a networked computer at Anytown base. Each of the operators makes a copy of the disc they created which is kept in an individual storage box within the office at Anytown.

When the office storage box is full (can contain up to 2yrs data), the discs are moved to an outside store at Anytown. There are other associated administration tasks that include statement writing and producing evidence.

Concentrations of Risk for the Camera Team.

1. All vehicles currently kept at the same base overnight. If access to base denied, significant impact after 24hrs.
2. Standalone computer at base compromised if access denied.
3. Majority of vehicles are of the same make, operation vulnerable if there is a manufacturer recall.
4. Team members store substantial amounts of data within the office, and more in a store at the same location, thus vulnerable to fire.

Suggested control measures.

1. Consider vehicle dispersal to other locations overnight.
2. Set up a second calibration area in another location.
3. Provide each of the team with a laptop that is capable of accessing the digital cameras from any location. May have software implication cost.
4. Over time, split the fleet, have two different makes of vehicle.
5. Reduce data stored in team office.
6. Relocate main data store away from base.

Report Conclusion

The principal vulnerabilities to this operation lie in the fact that all the activities are housed in the same building, making resilience poor. The suggested control measures outlined, would improve the team's ability to maintain a minimum level of service during a disruption at comparatively little cost.

Not everyone chooses to complete a report of this kind, however if you do, particularly if it is for another department, you will find it very useful.

There is a guide on how to complete a BIA in the "Templates" chapter, under Appendix C of the BC Policy.

6 THE ICT DEPARTMENT

"The ICT department is a strange country, they do things differently there" J. Ball & l. P. Hartley.

There are very few services provided within the Public Sector, that do not involve the use of information technology at some point in the process. By default, that makes the ICT department one of the most important sections of the organisation, and in my view one of the least understood by the business. This lack of understanding is slowly changing as more ICT literate executives take charge of the organisation.

If you are the BC Manager or Coordinator for a large organisation, you should make it your business to understand IT and how they work, better than anyone else. You will be astonished at how useful this knowledge will be to you.

Useful Tip. In order to develop this understanding, if it is at all possible, negotiate a three-month secondment to your ICT department, and in particular, if they have one, the continuous improvements unit. This is a big ask, and may not be viable in smaller organisations. If a secondment is unlikely, I recommend that you find a way to learn as much as you can about how things happen within ICT and how the systems that you use every day in your work are provided. It is a real eye opener. Secondly, whilst you are there, take some time to write their BC plan for them, they will be grateful for your expertise, and you will reap the benefits later.

Your knowledge of their plan will help you to assist the rest of the organisation in the development of their own plans.

ITIL 2011 – What's that?

ITIL is the acronym for the Information Technology Infrastructure Library, currently known as ITIL 2011. They are a collection of five volumes developed by the Cabinet Office and others that set out the best practice for the provision of IT services to meet business needs. If you are successful in getting a secondment to the ICT department, I would thoroughly recommend that you read these volumes, they will help you to understand "IT speak".

The language lexicon

When you start speaking to ICT, you may find that you will be using a different language, so it is important to have all parties understand the meaning of some frequently-used words, and the context in which they are used.

For instance, when you talk to most ICT people about business continuity, they will be thinking about disaster recovery (DR) – which to them is the same thing, and it can be, but in some cases, it isn't. Also DR can be about the recovery of a server, or the recovery of data from the cloud, plus a number of other things, which can confuse.

The term "Major incident" is very familiar to Police, fire ambulance and local authorities, and has a specific meaning, however a major incident in the ICT world can be quite different, so it is worth spending a bit of time making sure that you are talking about the same thing.

The Cabinet Office publish a very useful document called the Inter-agency Lexicon of UK Civil Protection Terminology, which is freely available on their website.

Application priorities

Your organisation will use hundreds of applications that the ICT department will keep going for you daily. By applications, I mean those end user products that are used by staff all the time and accessed via computer or laptop.

Microsoft Office, Outlook, Internet explorer, media player, building access control, and web-based programs, are all examples of "applications" used to conduct daily business.

Not all these applications will contribute to the running of time critical/prioritised activities, but the ones that do are quite important. For instance, telephony, network, email and communications are commonly considered as mainstay applications, but there will be others.

The ICT department will have some idea about what applications to protect and recover first after a disruption, but they will not know everything. It is therefore wise to pass on details gathered during the BIA about applications used for time critical activities, to the ICT department.

Useful Tip. Once the BIA is completed for the organisation and the list of applications is known, I would suggest you work with IT to develop a recovery priority system. The recovery timescales should be worked out with the ICT Department, but here is an example of what it could look like. For example, the most important could be priority 1, with a restoration time of 4hrs. The next important are priority 2 with a restoration time of 24hrs, followed by priority 3 with a restoration time of 48hrs and priority 4 with a restoration time of a week or more.

When this list has been agreed by the business and published, it will help to focus the ICT departments resources on what to recover first and inform everyone else which applications will be recovered and in what order.

Useful Tip. There is a lot of technical expertise in the ICT department, and I have often found that some key recovery skill has become the sole preserve of one person. This is of course a concentrated area of risk, and a single point of failure. A successful way to address this problem, is for each major application to have an operations manual that contains all relevant technical information that is required to recover it after a disruption. This means that anyone who understands the language, can do the work.

The Service Desk / Help Desk

Whatever the size of organisation, there is usually a service desk or help desk available that will give IT assistance to those staff that need it. Many of these service desks will aim to fix 75% of issues called in to them at the first point of contact. If the problem can't be solved on the first call, then it will be passed on to a second unit that will deal with it in slower time.

The service desk is a highly skilled environment and plays a key role in the successful day to day running of the business. Often, they will be the ones that will monitor and escalate technical issues to the relevant authorities and operate call out systems for staff. Without the service they provide, the organisation would cease to function very quickly.

Consequently, helping them to develop an BC plan early in the programme will produce great benefits and add resilience to the organisation.

Useful Tip. Whilst the Service Desk is susceptible to technical failures like everyone else, and should develop workarounds, their weakest point is generally their location. Finding an alternative location for the staff is very useful and remember, they don't all have to be together. Technology is advancing quickly, and with voice over internet protocol, very soon home working will be an option. Consider having a dispersal programme to your own or shared estate that is nearest to where staff live and use available hot desk areas.

Cyber Security

The prospect for 2018 is that cyber-attacks on organisations in the form of socially engineered emails that contain malware will continue and increase.

IT teams and system designers spend a lot of time trying to reduce the efficacy of these attacks by the improvement of IT security, which for the most part works reasonably well.

About 30% of disruptions that have been enabled are categorised as "Human Error".

This can occur where an unwitting member of staff lets in a virus by clicking on a rogue email or uses flash drives at work that have not been scanned for viruses.

It is inevitable that people will make mistakes, that fact is unavoidable. However, what I think we can do is to take action that will reduce the amount of times these mistakes occur. The way that we can do that is by educating our staff on what the problems are and how to avoid them.

IT is involved in all our lives and is here to stay. If we are to have any chance of reducing the human error factor by any margin at all, education and training must be more than a one-off session when you join the company.

I have set out a few ideas below that I think are low cost, easily achievable and would help to shut the door on easy access to our systems. The list is by no means exhaustive.

- Keep operating systems updated.
- Input to staff on cyber security when joining the organisation and twice yearly after that.
- Input on cyber security when staff are promoted or move section.
- Targeted input when real, relevant cyber events happen elsewhere.
- Cyber security responsibility put into staff development reports and made part of job description.
- Organisation information security dep't to run short education input via website, completion to be compulsory.
- Advice to staff on social engineering and phishing emails.
- Show staff YouTube videos on the subject – there are some good ones out there.
- Create a work environment where staff can confess quickly and without sanction if they do make a mistake.
- Advise staff on immediate actions if they think they have let a virus into the system.

I think that educating all staff in the benefits of cyber security should be a continuous process in the workplace. This kind of training has the potential to significantly reduce the amount of disruptions to our activities that are presently generated by human error.

Useful Tip. A video on YouTube called "The anatomy of an attack" is an excellent example of how emails are engineered to provide an attack vector into the company and helps to reinforce the message about not opening suspect emails.

7 THE BC PLAN

"No plan of operations extends with certainty beyond contact with the enemy's main strength" Field Marshall Helmut von Moltke the elder 1800 – 1891.

Before developing your BC plans it is worth taking some time to work out exactly what a plan is, and what you want it to achieve. When this idea is fixed in your mind it will help you through the process of developing a plan and keep you on track. There is some help available.

The Oxford English Dictionary defines a plan as "a plan of action designed to achieve a long term or overall aim".
ISO 22301:2012 3.6 describes a plan as" documented procedure's that guide organisations to respond, recover, resume, and restore to a pre-defined level of operations following disruption".

From these two descriptions you will agree that a plan must do something, it should take you somewhere, there must be an immediate benefit from having read it. At its most basic, a plan should answer these questions:
- What is it for?
- Who is it for?
- What do I do?

Plans should be simple, clear, up-to-date, and most importantly, short. This is the type of plan that will enable our member of staff to deliver a key service to someone who needs it at 2am. (Remember our two muses)

If it helps, you can think of this type of plan as your operational BC plan, although don't get bogged down with naming conventions, as they seem to be going out of fashion. Try not to expect too much from your plan, apart from the initial actions that are written in it, because once a disruption starts, things change quickly.

Helmut von Moltke the elder was well aware of this, a meticulous planner, he believed that the first engagement with the enemy was predictable. Consequently, he spent a great deal of time and care developing detailed plans that would guide his army through the early parts of a conflict.

He also understood that after the initial engagement everything could change, but at this point he relied on the training of his officers and men, and their understanding of his overall strategy. It was left to them to work out how these were to be achieved.

I think this is pretty much the same with a business continuity disruption. Once the plan has been activated, and you're at the fallback site, delivering your minimum level of service, the plan has done its work. Then your incident management teams and supervision will meet to work out what to do next.

How Many Plans?

The number of plans you end up with will vary according to the size and complexity of the organisation you work for. The Emergency Preparedness Manual suggests that it is a sound expedient for all departments to develop a BC plan to ensure day-to-day work is protected. So, you may have twenty to thirty plans by the time the programme is completed.

The majority of companies and organisations that I work with store their BC plans electronically and make them available to all staff, usually on some kind of file sharing setup like SharePoint. There are obvious dangers here of no access to plans during a network outage, so it is also wise to have relevant plans printed, or available via other formats.

Useful Tip. It is unlikely that your Executive Team are going to have the time to read any of these plans in depth but they will be keen on having an understanding what is in them, a paradox isn't it. To help with this it is worth developing a summary of all BC plans. This summary simply lists the departments, along with the time critical/prioritised activities they will be maintaining. It is also a very good strategic document to take to recovery meetings where Business Continuity activities may have to be re prioritised.

Fallback Locations

Finding somewhere else to put staff if their usual building is not available is becoming much more difficult than it used to be. A once estate rich Public Sector is reducing in size, and many areas are now sharing buildings to reduce the cost. This means that fallback locations need to be thought through very carefully, as there will be conflicting demands for the same space.

Hot desking and home working are very popular responses to the usual workplace being out of action and are a remedy. However, it is worth making sure that you have the IT infrastructure and laptop availability to service this remedy.

Useful Tip. If your organisation deals with an event, or disruption that is out of the ordinary, or even a major incident, it's worthwhile getting the ICT department to check how many people dialed into your systems remotely and check on the bandwidth use. If you do this over a period of time it will give you and ICT an idea of what bandwidth would be required if a lot of staff had to dial in from home.

Useful Tip. If any of your staff have been given an organisation laptop for work, make sure that they take it with them when they go home. Prevents embarrassment when there is no access to the building the next day.

Useful Tip. Some companies trawl their offices at night and collect all laptops that have been left behind, asking the owners for an explanation the following day. Harsh, but I'm told it works very well.

Plan Contents – what should be in it?

My initial response to the question "what should be in a plan?", is "only the information you need", the rest is a waste of printing, particularly in the type of plan we are dealing with now.

There is of course a more technical answer, and that lies within chapter 8.4.4 of ISO 22301, which lists all of the contents of a BC plan. There is also some generic information on the content and maintenance of plans in Annex 5D of chapter 5 of the Emergency Preparedness Manual which deals with Emergency Planning, that you may find useful.

BC Plan Template

Most large organisations within the Public Sector will already have a plan template that could be adapted for business continuity purposes, or failing that, a quick search on the internet will reveal hundreds of BC plan templates freely available for download.

I have added a plan template to the Templates chapter of this book, Appendix D of the BC Policy. The contents of the plan template fall generally in line with the guidance in ISO22301 that you can use if you wish. I have no doubt that there are better templates out there, but I do know that this one works.

I will go through the template headings and layout in this chapter, which I hope will assist you when you come to filling it out.

The first two pages are self-explanatory.

Page 3

On page 3 of the template you will find a chart entitled "Activation Criteria". This chart provides an uncomplicated guide as to when to activate the plan. Moving from left to right across the chart, you can see that local management arrangements will apply up to a certain point. The kind of things dealt with on a day-to-day basis by supervisors such as staff calling in sick, the possibility of some staff being late, or some needing to go early, would not be a reason to activate your BC plan.

But when these problems escalate, say half of your team are sick with a virus, then there will be other things to consider, and activating your plan may be one of them.

The wording in the chart is a generic example which you can change to suit your needs.

Page 4

Entitled "Critical/Prioritised Activity 1" this page is where you set out your BC solutions to each disruption for a particular activity. If your solutions are the same for a number of your critical/prioritised activities, then put them all in the same list at the top of the page. Don't duplicate the forms for the sake of it.

Minimum BC objective (MBCO): Detail the minimum level of service that this activity will deliver, and the minimum staff required.

Recovery Time Objective(RTO): Detail what the recovery time objective is for this activity.

Recovery Procedures: Detail the recovery procedures, actions and tasks per risk. Also detail the resources required to deliver your minimum level of service recovery. Consider fall-back site, equipment, communications, data management, PPE, records, security, internal / external dependencies / suppliers if any.

The decision to invoke this Continuity Plan will be a matter of professional judgement; in any case the process must be started in sufficient time to ensure that the objectives are met.

The next part of the form deals with your solutions to various types of disruption that may occur. I will fill out the fallback element as an example.

Building Not Available: **Fall-back Site Location:** Location here.

Activate Fall-back Site

1. Evacuate building
2. Contact team and advise of fallback procedure in motion.
3. Contact senior manager and advice re plan activation
4. Advise communications staff of new location
5. Etc

Fall-back Resources Information:

1. There are 15 desks and computers available at the fallback site for the team
2. Parking is free within the site if staff go by car
3. There are kitchen and toilet facilities on the same floor as the fallback offices.
4. Etc

Follow the same format for the rest of the list. Actions first followed by resource availability. This will help to keep your plan simple and straightforward.

Pages 5,6,7

These pages contain additional forms as on page 4, delete them if not required.

Page 8,9,10

Plan Description: This Plan represents *insert department name* arrangements to ensure that it can deliver essential services in line with organisational priorities.

Scope: Detail the scope of the plan.

This plan assumes that we may be unable to provide Departmental services in the normal way, perhaps through severe staff shortages or loss of primary accommodation. It contains arrangements to provide a minimum level of service, and provisions for alternative working practices and locations that will ensure the time critical activities of the Department can be maintained during a disruption.

Purpose: Detail the purpose of the plan.

This plan describes the methods by which the *insert department name* will maintain our critical activities when faced with an incident that may impact significantly on delivery of normal services for a protracted period.

Risks to Delivery: List the most likely risks to delivery, this list can change according to the type of activity being delivered.

- Loss of access to main buildings
- Substantial reduction in staff, key personnel
- Loss of IT systems, telecommunications, data, information
- Loss of electrical power, water supply, fuel
- Loss of key supplier / specialist equipment

Command Structure and Responsibilities: The structure below sets out the format that will be used to command all *insert department name* BC disruptions.

"You may feel that the Gold, Silver Bronze structure is too formalised for your departmental BC plan command and will confuse other staff used to this structure in larger incidents. If that is the case, you should change the template to suit your needs."

Incident Management Team for *insert department name* **Department:** Insert the names of the staff in your department that will take on the roles of Gold, Silver and Bronze.

Incident Management Room / Location: Identify a location or locations where the incident will be managed from. This will be the focal point for all activity during the disruption. Depending on the size of your organisation, a second alternative may be worthwhile.

Gold: (insert name) Head of *insert department name* Department has overall strategic responsibility for the business continuity response and recovery phases. Suggested Task List in Annex D.

Silver: (insert name/s) are the senior management team for *department name* Department and are responsible for the tactics for delivery of departmental critical activities, management of the ongoing recovery process and communications with Gold. Suggested Task List in Annex D.

Bronze/s: (insert name/s) will form the Bronze team/s that will recover the critical activity that has been lost and manage the delivery of a minimum level of service to its pre-determined level. Suggested Task List in Annex D.

Plan Activation: Who can activate the plan, when and how? Change the text below to suit your own plan.

This plan, or any part of it, may be invoked either by Organisation Gold or any of (*department name*) departments senior management team in circumstances where they believe that it is not possible to continue to deliver these functions in the normal way and the consequences are such that it may have significant implications for the delivery of normal operations for a protracted period.

The decision to invoke this Continuity Plan will be a matter of professional judgement; in any case the process must be started in sufficient time to ensure that the recovery priorities are met.

To assist in this decision-making process, a plan activation chart has been provided on page 3.

Considerations-The person invoking the Continuity Plan should:

- Consider immediate staff welfare requirements / evacuation if appropriate
- If out of hours, consider activating the
- communications plan Annex A
- Assess the extent of the disruption and confirm the need to invoke this plan using the Activation Criteria chart on page 3.
- Commence incident / decision log.
- Refer to the most relevant recovery plan for the situation encountered
- Call out the relevant Duty Manager – use appropriate call out system for org.
- Consider informing Organisation Gold Commander.

- Consider contacting organisation Media relations staff
- Retain Command and Control until the arrival of the Senior Manager
- Consider appointing supervisors / team leaders for bronze functions e.g. key skills and logistics

The Head of (*department name*) **Department or their Deputy, once informed, will be responsible for continuity arrangements. They will:**

- Assume the role of Gold (Continuity), except in circumstances where there is, or is potential for, organisation - wide impact, in which case management of the incident will be the responsibility of Organisation Gold or Executive Officer.
- In these circumstances, they will assume the role of Silver. Gather information, assess the extent of the disruption and confirm the need to invoke this plan.
- Open a decision / Policy log
- If the disruption is wide-ranging, liaise with Organisational Gold, asses the need to invoke any other relevant or related plans.

Recovery Phase: When the immediate effects of the incident have been overcome, execute detailed site evaluation, if required. Depending on the size and nature of the disruption, recovery can be complex and may involve more agencies than were used in the response phase e.g. facilities, estates, IT dept.

After a major disruption consider the following actions:

- Ensure a strategy is in place to inform any displaced staff of new working arrangements and to support staff welfare.
- Determine period for which buildings (or part thereof) may be uninhabitable. Obtain a professional assessment where appropriate
- Determine any temporary arrangements / accommodation to assist the recovery phase
- Identify and provide for any special security arrangements resulting from personnel relocation
- Reassess the recovery plan on a regular basis
- Develop and implement a stand-down plan at the appropriate time to ensure a smooth transition to normality.

A localised disruption may be less impactive and so recovered more easily using departmental structures and resources.

Standing down: Standing down from a Business Continuity Incident will be at the discretion of the Organisation Level Recovery Team or the Head of the affected department / Duty Manager if the incident is more localised.

Pages 10,11,12,13

There are a number of annexes at the end of the template which includes a communications plan for your team and an incident management team agenda, should you have to put a meeting together.

These are only suggestions, so change them to suit your circumstances and preferences.

Annex A

Internal Communications Plan

There are any number of reasons that could result in staff working from home or another location within the organisation area. The most likely causes are Influenza, Norovirus, severe weather, or usual place of work not available.

This plan has been set up to maintain communications with staff working under those conditions, when we cannot communicate with them in the usual way.

It is important to have an uncomplicated way of communicating with staff during a disruption or when dispersed that is accessible to all. The following suggestions are not the only way this can be done but is designed to give you some ideas that might suit you and the way your team works.

1. A simple list of all the teams contact numbers kept by managers / team leaders – personal numbers should not be published within the plan.
2. A snapshot of organisation phone list may be downloaded onto managers work mobiles.
3. Depending on organisations arrangements with Microsoft, you may be able to use "Outlook" to send your team a group text message. You may already have a bulk messaging system that can be utilised.
4. Make a page of your outward facing website accessible to staff, where you can publish advice and guidance during a disruption.

5. Set up a Public Sector BT Meetme account that will allow managers to contact staff via a conference call. The set-up cost is free to the Public Sector, but there is a cost for calls.
6. Prior to any disruption, if you have Office 365, set up a group within Microsoft Lync that can be used to message the team as a group. Also, if the team are dispersed and using laptops, Lync can be used for video conferencing.

The communications plan can be activated under these conditions:

- If for any reason a disruption is expected, then staff can be warned in advance that they will be working elsewhere, and the communications plan will be activated on a given date.
- In the event of an unexpected disruption, such as power outage or fire, the duty manager / team leader will inform staff using the preferred communications method in this plan.

Plan Execution (This is a suggested format. Change it as you see fit or delete entirely.)

- 0800 – Senior management team (SMT) / duty manager conduct conference call to discuss: a. department strategy during the disruption, b. staff issues, c. incidents, d. department messages, e. other subjects as required.
- 0830- All managers / team leaders to call in on the conference call for a briefing from SMT or their representative.

- 0900 – Managers / team leaders host conference call with staff that are working from home or alternative locations and communicate messages from 0800 meeting. All other staff will be informed using usual methods of communication if they are available.
- 1530 – Managers / team leaders host conference call with staff that are working from home or alternative locations, pick up staff issues, and incidents arising during the day.
- 1600 – Senior management team / duty manager conduct conference call to pick up on issues fed back by staff to managers / team leaders and set agenda / actions for following day's 0800 conference.

Annex B

Telephone Contact List

Name. Role. Contact No.

Annex C Incident Management Team
Suggested Agenda

The suggestions for these agenda items are based on the Joint Emergency Services Interoperability Programme (JESIP) Joint Decision Model, which is a tried and tested way of approaching decisions. Printed by kind permission of the Joint Emergency Services programme.

Gather information and intelligence

- Introductions (roles/responsibilities) - Identify individual to record actions
- Any items requiring urgent attention - Take action where needed
- Situation report – reason for plan activation -
- Update from all departments -

Assess risks and develop a working strategy

- Assess impact on staff and review welfare / health and safety
- Assess likely recovery time - Prioritise recovery of services if required
- Assess impact on critical services - List critical activities affected
- Assess impact on related activities - There will be some services interrelated with critical activities.
- Develop or review initial working strategy – If a large disruption, refer to organisation strategy.

Consider powers, policies and procedures

- If organisation wide – agree areas of responsibility with crisis team
- Consider areas of responsibility – appoint Bronzes as required.
- Identify relevant policies, legislation and procedures – Finance, Estates, HR.

Identify options and contingencies

- Review current actions on recovery of critical activities – may need to be prioritised
- Consider if additional actions are required to prevent further loss of service.

- Consider options based on circumstances and not covered in the BC plan.
- Consider additional contingencies should disruption escalate – identify and prepare.
- Consider internal and external communications messages to staff and interested parties.
- Are the right people at this meeting – who else should attend?
- Consider mutual aid from other departments / organisations / voluntary sector / partners.
- Are all actions and decisions supported by the company ethos, ethics and codes of practice?
- Any other business – Time and location of next meeting

Take action and review what happened
- Close meeting – Implement actions
- If organisation wide – give update to organisation Crisis Team
- Ensure update on actions is available for next meeting.

Annex D   Additional Task Lists

This annex can be used to contain any additional task lists that you may feel are relevant to your plan that will assist or guide those who have tasks within it. If there are none, then delete.

Annex E   Evacuation and Welfare Details

This annex can be used to contain any evacuation and welfare arrangements that have been made for staff in the event of a disruption. It may also contain details of any specific arrangements for staff who have existing disabilities, temporary disabilities, or other issues that require reasonable adjustments to be made.

Annex F   Associated Business Continuity Plans

This annex can be used to contain the details of any existing business continuity plans that are linked or associated to this one and may be of use during a disruption. If other BC plans are directly linked, ie, one plan cannot be activated without the other, then details of its activation should be included in the body of your plan. If they are associated, then the location of those plans should be noted here.

Page 14

This page contains the administration for the plan, which often is in the first few pages of most documents. I have put it at the back because it is the last thing that you want to see when trying to find out what to do and activate your plan. However, you may want to add the version number and last review date of the plan to the front page.

8 TRAINING AND EXERCISING

"Error is indispensable to the process of discovery". Mathew Syed.

A plan is not a plan until it has been validated with an exercise. Chapter 6, paragraph 6.22 of the Emergency Preparedness manual states "the regulations require Category 1 responders to put into place arrangements for exercising BC plans to ensure that they are effective."

Note 1 of the definition of an exercise in 3.18 of ISO22301 has a very helpful list of what exercises can be used for: "validating policies, plans, procedures, training, equipment and inter organisational agreements; clarifying and training personnel in roles and responsibilities; improving inter organisational coordination and communications; identifying gaps in resources; improving individual performance; and identifying opportunities for improvement, and controlled opportunity to practice improvisation".

Far too many people see exercises as having an implied pass or a fail, when in fact they are a rehearsal, a familiarisation and most importantly an opportunity for learning. A test has an implied pass or fail. So, we test equipment and systems, and exercise people.

Training

Before you subject your staff to the stresses and strains of an exercise it is important that they have had some training and awareness on their roles within the plan. Exercising is not designed to catch people out; it tests procedures, not people. If staff are under prepared through lack of training, they will not get the best learning from the exercise and will quickly loose interest.

An important aim in running an exercise is to make people feel more comfortable in their roles and identify lessons for the future. It is also important that senior personnel are committed to exercising. They too must be practiced in their role and up to date with changes in procedures.

Exercises have four main objectives:

- To validate plans (verify that plans work)
- To develop and familiarise key staff in carrying out their roles (training / rehearsal)
- To test equipment and systems.
- To identify gaps in processes, training and policies.

Most exercises should aim to achieve all or at least some elements of these objectives.

Plan exercising.

If you are a Category 1 responder, you may find it helpful to carry out multi agency exercising where possible. Get your Local Resilience Forum Management Team involved who can help to coordinate the exercise between their partner agencies. Exercising with others can produce important lessons that would otherwise be missed during a single agency exercise.

The best way to exercise everyone's plan in the organisation is to have a yearlong programme of exercises. When you combine these planned events with any real time plan activations that have occurred, you will have quite a list.

I used to meet with our BC Coordinators every three months, and an agenda item for that meeting was a planned exercise, which had to be completed by the next meeting. These were not full-blown exercises of all their plans every three months, sometimes it would be a small element of their plan that was looked at. The type of exercise would depend on what was going on in the real world. For instance, if part of the organisation had suffered a network outage, I would get all the organisations plans looked at for a response to that type of event.

Useful Tip. Make up an exercise calendar on a spreadsheet for all your departments so that you can keep a record of exercises and plan activations. It will come in useful when your programme has matured, and you start to develop key performance indicators.

Plan testing.

The elements of a business continuity plan that can be tested are as follows:

- Plan activation process
- Communications
- Any setting up procedures
- Staff contact lists

The plan activation process can be examined by running a short test, in which the staff responsible for triggering plan activation are asked to do so. This should be done at least annually.

The communications methods used to contact staff during a disruption can be tested regularly. Some organisations have formed groups using social media apps like "Whats App", which are very useful. However, be careful with these, particularly with the type of information you put out there.

The setting up procedures for control centres and other key facilities should be tested at leas annually. This includes provision of necessary premises, emergency supplies and equipment and ensuring they can be located quickly and placed in the right positions where they are needed.

Confirming the numbers and details on staff contact lists can also be done on a regular basis.

Useful Tip. Do not publish the private numbers of your staff on your plan. This can lead to all kinds of problems. If you are not able to provide key personnel with a company phone, find a secure way for supervisors to have access to these details outside of the organisations main systems.

Exercise type.

There are four main types of exercise:

- Seminar / syndicate based
- exercises
- Table top

- Command post
- Live Play

The choice of which of the following exercise types to adopt depends on a number of considerations including:
- What you want to achieve
- How much is in the budget
- How much time do you have

A discussion based / seminar exercise is cheapest to run and easiest to prepare. Often based on a completed plan in which the participants are divided into groups and discuss the plan in a non-pressurised environment.

Table top exercises are a simple, cost effective way of exercising plans. They are commonly used where the discussion is based on a relevant scenario with a time line that is controlled with time injects that develops the exercise in real time.

In this type of exercise, the players are expected to be familiar with their own plans and are expected to demonstrate how these plans work as the scenario unfolds.

Media can be involved, which adds to the efficacy of the period. They provide the players with an excellent opportunity to interact with and understand the roles of the other agencies taking part.

A command post exercise is cost effective and does not require the use of front line staff. The team leaders and communications teams from each participating organisation are positioned in the locations they would use during an actual incident or live exercise. This tests communication arrangements and the flow of information between players from participating organisations.

A live exercise can be the best way of confirming the efficacy of a plan and its communications. The size and complexity of the plan will dictate the amount of planning and costs that will be incurred. Apart from fire drills, which are by necessity a live play activity, I would use either a table top or seminar event to exercise Business Continuity plans.

Exercise frequency

Business continuity Plans should be exercised at the very least once a year or after a major organisation change. I think annually is not frequent enough because things change much quicker than that. I much prefer smaller exercises quarterly, it keeps the plans up to date and keeps the subject of BC in the air with the organisation.

Lessons identified

Whatever type of exercise you use, at the end of it, there will have been some lessons identified that require action. It is important for the development of your business continuity plan that these are followed up and actioned.

Equally after a live activation of your plan for a real disruption, do the same thing, conduct a post incident review, pick up lessons identified and update your plan. This will allow the plan to develop organically, and because it has been exposed to real time events, it will be all the better for it, and much more effective. Remember, there is hidden value in failure.

For more detailed information on planning exercises, the cabinet office has produced "The Exercise Planners Guide" which is freely available from their website.

Exercise scenarios

If you plan an exercise, whatever type it is, keep the scenario simple. I have experienced a considerable number of live disruptions with varying levels of impact, and common to them all is that cause was usually something very simple.

For example, building access denial caused by being inside a cordon put on a separate building by Fire and Rescue, 3ft watermain breached by workmen, power cables dug up by road works, Call Centre 101 calls in the South of England disrupted by a server failure in Birmingham. The list goes on.

A simple scenario will keep the players grounded, and willing to apply themselves to the problems you set.

I have put a number of exercise scenarios in Chapter 12 for your use, which are based on real events and caused plans to be activated.

Piggyback opportunities

Within most Category 1 responder organisations, there is nearly always some kind of exercising going on, usually Emergency Planning. If you discover an exercise is being planned for your area, contact the exercise planners and get them to write in a Business Continuity element to the exercise, and put you on the planning team.

This will add a realistic dimension to the exercise, and get people thinking about BC at the same time. The added bonus is that it will encourage the exercise players to read their BC plans as well.

9 PROMOTING BC TO THE ORGANISATION

"Educating the mind without educating the heart, is no education at all". Aristotle 384BC

Why?

Paragraph 6.93 of chapter 6 in the Emergency Preparedness Manual recommends "an education and awareness programme for both internal and external stakeholders". whilst in paragraph 7.3 of ISO22301 "awareness" is the watchword.

In both cases there is a hint that an education programme should developed around BC for the entire organisation.

If you are starting this programme from scratch, I would allow a five-year plan to get BC properly rooted into the organisation. Having done all the work, and written the plans, the aim now is to make BC part of the way you do business, and the only way you can do that is by education.

This part of the process isn't easy, and it is important to understand that pay is not the only motivator for the workforce. Staff will also have differing levels of intellectual and emotional buy in to the organisations goals and aspirations.

You will come across four categories of staff that you have to deal with, they are:

- 30% Champions – they have both intellectual and emotional buy in.
- 31% Loose cannons and Bystanders – have one or the other but not both.

- 39% Weak links – do not care about the company strategy or their role in implementing it.

These are chilling numbers and demonstrate what you will be up against. I think it is also fair to say that staff will move from one category to the other over time, and back again, so it's not all gloom. The aim is to catch them when they are in the Champions area.

How?

Your organisation will already have some existing methods that are used to communicate with staff. Intranet messaging pages, notice boards, priority messaging systems, staff email and routine publications that carry organisational news. These are a good place to start the conversation. I have already mentioned annual staff surveys on Business Continuity which will also push the message.

Here are a few more ideas that have worked for me in the past:

- Information package for staff new to the company. It needn't be a complicated message, but one that explains the organisations commitment to BC.
- Get on to any project that is introducing new IT systems into the organisation and make sure there is a BC element to the delivery of it.
- Run a media campaign for a set period every year.
- BC themed computer wallpaper.
- Posters – these can be downloaded from the Business Continuity Institute website for free – or make up your own.
- If you are a Police force, make sure that your Police and Crime Commissioner's office has a BC plan.

- Contingency planning – make sure that there is a BC element to any organisational contingency or operational plans that are commonly used.
- Procurement process – make sure that there is a BC element in the procurement process for outside suppliers, particularly those suppling services to a time critical activity.
- Messages from Chief Executives
- Staff appraisals and development reports – BC should feature in all staff reports that are relevant.
- Job Descriptions – Those staff with a responsibility for BC should have that articulated in their job description

Because you are aiming to change the culture of the business, it is important to think these promotional messages through carefully. Be consistent, persistent and ever present. You will know the message is getting through when staff are contacting you about Business Continuity, and not the other way around.

When?

International Business Continuity Awareness Week (BCAW), promoted worldwide by the Business Continuity Institute and takes place in May. I found this to be a perfect time to promote some of the activities I have mentioned above to the organisation.

Useful Tip. I you decide to use BCAW to promote BC, get your media campaign arranged beforehand, and start it off with a message from the Chief Officer or Chief Executive to all staff about the importance of Business Continuity. This is very effective and sets the right tone for the rest of the week.

Use every opportunity you can in order to get the message out.

10 CONTINUAL IMPROVEMENTS

"Governance is the system of rules, practices and processes by which an organisation is directed and controlled"

Governance

In aligning to the BC standard, the organisation is committing itself to absorbing Business Continuity into its existing business management practices. Consequently, you will need the following for this to work:

- Someone from the Executive Group, a Deputy Chief Officer or Deputy Chief Executive to have vicarious liability for BC, in other words a BC Champion at the top table.
- A governing board for BC. This would be a natural fit for some kind of Risk Board or group that is responsible for operational matters. This group will deal with BC issues on an organisation wide basis that cannot be dealt with locally.
- A BC Coordinator who will report into the executive board.
- A BC Representatives group chaired by the BC Coordinator who will take issues that cannot be dealt with locally to the Executive Board, as well as pass on decisions from the Executive Group for dispersal across the organisation.

Whatever organisation you work for, there will be an existing system of governance that will accommodate Business Continuity and form your BC Management system.

Key performance Indicators (KPIs)

As your BC programme develops and gains maturity, the question of performance indicators and monitoring will arise. Most organisations will have some kind of performance monitoring board, often chaired by senior officers, that will want to know how BC is doing. The need for this knowledge is driven by the fact that BC is a legislated duty, and so audit information will be required and BC is an important contributor to organisation resilience.

When I set up an evaluation system, I produced a spreadsheet with the following headings that I monitored and reported on quarterly:

- Total departments
- Total with plans
- Total without plans
- Total new plans expected this year
- Total plans reviewed
- Expected reviews this year
- Total plans exercised
- Expected plans exercised this year
- Total BC Reps trained annually
- Total BC Reps trained overall
- Total live plan activations this year

In order to measure the performance of BC you will have to set some kind of target for the year. For example, plans should be reviewed and tested at least once per year, so it would be a reasonable target to set.

You will find that senior managers do not want to fall below expectations as far as targets for their area of work go, so will be keen to assist you in overcoming any obstacles that you may be experiencing by way of getting your job done.

Horizon Scanning

Horizon scanning is an integral part of effective Business Continuity Management and should be carried out pretty much continuously. The best analogy I could come up with is the driverless car, where in order to not crash into anything, it must constantly analyse real time data and take the necessary action to stay on course.

In his book, Superforcasting: The art and Science of Prediction, Philip E Tetlock reinforces the idea of constantly updating and assessing data, and changing the prediction accordingly based on the newest information. An engaging read, which I would thoroughly recommend.

"How do I horizon scan?" I hear you ask. Well, before I can explain what works for me, you have to read the segment of the poem below, because I think it presents a perfect mind-set with which to approach horizon scanning. It is part of a sonnet, so won't take long.

Leisure by W.H. Davies

What is this life if, full of care,
We have no time to stand and stare.
No time to stand beneath the boughs
And stare as long as sheep or cows.
No time to see, when woods we pass,
Where squirrels hide their nuts in grass.
No time to see, in broad daylight,
Streams full of stars, like skies at night.
A poor life this if, full of care,
We have no time to stand and stare.

For me, horizon scanning is about taking time to stand and stare, to take a step back from the daily routines and have a look around. We very often look but don't see – do you know the colour of your partner's eyes for instance? Some will know, but many wont.

Try this experiment in looking and seeing, (and it doesn't matter if you can draw or not) – simply take 10 minutes to draw an object from real life. I will guarantee that once complete, you will have "seen" more of what that object really looks like in all of its detail.

My grandad used to say "never buy a car in the rain" (they always look better wet) and "always polish a new car the day you get it". (you will find all the scratches you missed when you first looked). It's all about seeing what you're looking at.

Apart from keeping an eye on world events all the time, I used to spend a couple of hours every Monday morning horizon scanning around the world. If you sign up to "Continuity Central" they will send you a weekly and monthly Business Continuity newsletter that contains articles from all over the world. It can be a bit like sifting through mud, but occasionally you are left with a diamond that you can use.

So, next Monday, when you're horizon scanning, take time to stand and stare, to look and really see what's happening in the world and around you. This will help you to spot the juggernaut that's heading in your direction and possibly present an early opportunity to jump on board, get out of the way, defend against it or exploit the situation.

11 BC TEMPLATES

"Things done well, and with a care, exempt themselves from fear"
William Shakespeare.

Note: whilst this book is aimed at BC practitioners in the Public Sector, the broad principles can be applied to all types of organisations. I have therefore added in italics, considerations which apply to the Public Sector only.

Template 1. Business Continuity Policy Template
Introduction

This Policy advocates the development and maintenance of Business Continuity plans that as far as is practicable, enable *insert company or organisation name here* can continue to carry out and maintain time critical services in the event of an emergency in compliance with the Civil Contingencies Act 2004 (CCA 2004*).*

Compliance with the CCA 2004 does not apply if you are a private company. You may choose to align yourself with the BCI Good Practice Guidelines or the international standards for Business Continuity ISO22301/313.

Scope

This Policy and associated appendices provide comprehensive guidance on how to develop and maintain Business Continuity plans. See also the individual scopes of specific plans found at Appendices D of this policy.

Policy Statement

Insert company or organisation name here will apply this process to all areas of the business to determine those activities that are time critical to the continued delivery of our strategic objectives. *If you are Public Sector add" and meet our duties under the act, CCA 2004."* We recognise / intend to comply with / the principles within the International Organisation for Standardisation (ISO 22301) for Business Continuity, which will be used to benchmark our BC activities and success.

(Procedure) Introduction

If you are Public Sector, use this. The Civil Contingencies Act places a duty on......name your service, police, ambulance etc..... as a category 1 responder to produce plans that ensure they can continue to carry out their respective functions and maintain time critical/prioritised services to a pre-determined level in the event of an emergency.

This Policy is the key document which sets out the scope and governance of Business Continuity Management (BCM) in *name your company or department here*. It provides the context in which BCM will be developed to ensure that it supports the objectives and culture of our organisation, and includes:

- Scope of the BCM programme
- BCM framework and responsibilities
- BCM guidelines and standards

This Policy will be reviewed every *put in the timescale here, should be at least annually* or after any major disruption or reorganisation. (Auditors will check this)

Terms and Definitions

A list of terms and definitions used in this Policy are in Appendix A.

This appendix should contain all of the acronyms used in the Policy and its appendices.

Relationship with Organisation Risk Process

The Risk Management process in *put organisation name or department here* provides the primary mechanisms for identification, analysis and control of operational and strategic business risks. Business Continuity Management supports this in the following ways:

- Through the impact analysis of the loss or disruption to a time critical/prioritised activity that supports our core business objectives.
- Through the planning undertaken to enable the restoration of time critical activities to a pre-determined level within an agreed time scale.
- Through the identification of risks to these activities that may need a business decision to resolve.

Strategic Objectives / Core Business

The strategic objectives / core business for *insert company name or department here* are:

- Protection of life and vulnerable people
- *Next objective*
- *Next objective*
- *Next objective*
- *Next objective*

These objectives should reflect the activities that you do not want to stop; they are your principal reasons why your organisation exists.

Aim

Using the Business Continuity process to ensure that as far as is practicable we can carry out our strategic objectives / core business activities in the event of an emergency or disruption.

BC Process Objectives

- Identify those activities and processes critical to our strategic objectives / core business.
- Understand the impact of their disruption or loss
- Anticipate and mitigate risks to their delivery
- Produce validated flexible plans that restore disrupted activities to a pre-determined level.

BC Plan Scope

BC plans will define the scope of the incidents that they are designed to address, and will take account of those disruptions most likely to impact time critical activities:

- Loss of access to key building
- Substantial reduction in staff
- Loss of IT systems, telecommunications
- Loss of data, information, vital records
- Loss of utilities, supply chain

Most scenarios will affect one of the broad categories above, however you can add anything that is relevant to the delivery of your activity, e.g. specialist equipment.

Benefits

The application of this Policy will reflect our alignment to ISO22301/313. *Public Sector. – will ensure compliance with the duties set out in CCA 2004*

The implementation of this Policy will enable *organisation name here* to:

- Identify, mitigate and manage risks to strategic objectives / core business
- Improve our ability to deal with, and recover from a disruption
- Provide our key services during a disruption

Roles and Responsibilities

There are specific responsibilities for the roles listed below which are detailed in Appendix B of this Policy.

- *Name the governing board for Business Continuity*
- *Name of Executive who is responsible for BC*
- *Name of BC Manager or Coordinator*
- *Heads of business units and departments*
- *Business Continuity Representatives*
- *Line Managers*
- *Staff*

There may be other headings for BC responsibilities that you would like to name here, but they should be set out in detail in the appendix and agreed by the organisation executive board.

Business Continuity Planning Process

The Business Continuity process, and planning template that we intend to follow is set out in Appendix C of this Policy. Part 1 of which, will guide you through the details of the planning process. Once completed, the information gathered in part 1 can be used to complete part 2, which is the Business Continuity plan template, which can also be found in Appendix D to this Policy.

Use this appendix to set out a method of achieving a BC plan. The people that use this information will need to have received some basic training in BC and would usually be the person responsible for writing the plan. For details on training contact ***johnball@bcfundamentals.com***

Collaborative Plans

Public Sector. Where there are any teams working across collaborative areas they will develop joint plans that will improve the resilience of the group as a whole and cover all applicable areas.

Completed Business Continuity Plans

Once plans have been completed and signed off by the appropriate authority they should be validated by exercise, then made available to staff.

All plans should be exercised at least once per year, or after major organisational change.

Debriefing and update

All plan activations and exercises should be debriefed by an appropriate person with the express aim of identifying areas of success and areas that require improvement within the plan and changing the plan accordingly.

Policy Template Appendix A – Terms and Definitions

Business Continuity (BC)

Capability of the organisation to continue delivery of products or services at acceptable predefined levels following a disruptive incident. (ISO 22301,2012 3.3)

Business Continuity Management (BCM)

Holistic management process that identifies potential threats to an organisation and the impacts to business operations those threats, if realised, might cause, and which provides a framework for building organisational resilience with the capability of an effective response that safeguards the interest of its interested parties, reputation, brand and value creating activities. (ISO 22301,2012 3.4).

Business Continuity Management System (BCMS)

Part of the overall management system that establishes, implements, operates, monitors, reviews, maintains and improves Business Continuity. (ISO 22301,2012 3.5)

Business Continuity Plan

Documented procedures that guide organisations to respond, recover, resume, and restore to a pre-defined level of operation following a disruption. (ISO 22301,2012 3.6)

Business Impact Analysis (BIA)

The process of analysing activities and the effect that a business disruption might have on them. (Source ISO 22301,2012 3.8).

Maximum Acceptable Outage (MAO) and Maximum Tolerable Period of Disruption (MTPD)

The time it would take for adverse impacts, which might arise as a result of not providing a product / service or performing an activity, to become unacceptable. (ISO 22301,2012 3.25 / 3.26)

Minimum Business Continuity Objective (MBCO)
Minimum level of services and or products that is acceptable to the organisation to achieve its business objectives during a disruption. (ISO 22301,2012 3.28)

Recovery Point Objective (RPO)
Point to which information used by an activity must be restored to enable the activity to operate on resumption. (ISO 22301,2012 3.44) (Usually this refers to the amount of data that can be recovered when a computer system fails. The level of IT support that each system receives will govern this objective.)

Recovery Time Objective (RTO)
The period of time following an incident within which a service or activity must be resumed, or resource recovered. (ISO 22301,2012 3.45) This time must be less than MAO or MTPD.

Policy
The intentions and direction of an organisation as formally expressed by its top management. (ISO 22301,2012 3.38)
Exercise
Process to train for, assess, practice and improve performance in an organisation.

Note 1. Exercises can be used for: validating policies, plans, procedures, training, equipment and inter organisational agreements; clarifying and training personnel in roles and responsibilities; improving inter organisational coordination and communications; identifying gaps in resources; improving individual performance; and identifying opportunities for improvement, and controlled opportunity to practice improvisation.

Note 2. A test is a unique and particular type of exercise, which incorporates an expectation of a pass or a fail element within the goal or objectives of the exercise being planned. (ISO 22301,2012 3.18)

Policy Template Appendix B – Roles and Responsibilities

The terms that I have used in describing roles and responsibilities may not be the ones that your organisation uses. However, it is likely that you will have similar groups, so change the roles accordingly.

1. Corporate Management Group
- This group is responsible for defining and directing the strategic approach to BCM across insert your company name here.
- This group will ensure that effective and robust Business Continuity practices and procedures are in place across the organisation / business.

2. Corporate Risk Management Group

- This group is the executive group responsible for defining and directing the strategic approach to risk across the organisation area in accordance with the Risk Management strategy.
- This group will have tactical responsibility for Business Continuity across our area and will make decisions on any risks identified by the Business Continuity process that cannot be resolved at a local level.

3. Operational Lead / BC Coordinator

The Operational Lead / BC Coordinator will: -

- Work with managers to ensure that all time critical activities are identified, and Business Continuity Plans are developed.
- Monitor and benchmark the testing of Business Continuity Plans on an annual basis.
- Provide training and professional advice to support managers in the development, implementation and testing of Business Continuity Plans.
- Be responsible for ensuring that any lessons learned or identified from testing or activation of any Business Continuity plans are shared with other departments and reported to the Corporate Management Group or the Risk Management group as required.
- Chair the Business Continuity Group quarterly meetings.

4. Assistant Directors

Assistant Directors will:

- Enable the production of effective Business Continuity Plans/resumption plans where appropriate.
- Enable the reviewing of the Business Continuity Plans/resumption plans at least annually.
- Promote the exercising and evaluation of its Business Continuity Plan(s) at least once a year.
- Nominate a Business Continuity Representative, who will be responsible for the development, writing, annual review and testing process of the Business Continuity plans.

- Ensure that the Business Continuity Representatives are adequately trained.

5. Senior Managers

Senior Managers will support the Operational Lead / BC Coordinator to:

- Work with their teams to ensure that all time critical activities are identified, and Business Continuity Plans developed.
- Monitor and benchmark the testing of Business Continuity Plans on an annual basis.
- Be responsible for ensuring that any lessons learned or identified from testing or activation of any Business Continuity plans are shared with other departments and reported to the Corporate Management Group or the Risk Management Group.
- Support the Business Continuity planning process and testing activity.
- Provide staff with the opportunity to acquaint themselves with the organisations BC arrangements.
- Ensure that all staff within their charge are made aware of any Business Continuity Plans that may affect them.

6. Staff Members
- All staff members should read any Business Continuity plan that is relevant to their area of business and be familiar with their part in it.

Policy Template Appendix C – Business Impact Analysis -: Practical Guide

Introduction
This guide has been developed to assist those who have been given the task of producing a Business Continuity Plan. It is operationally focussed and scalable, so can be adapted to suit a large multi-functional area of business or a smaller unit. All the principles involved in developing a plan are the same.

The guidance in this document is a pared down practical view of BC, which can be studied in detail by reading the International standard for BC, ISO22301 / 22313.

Assumptions
In developing this guide, several assumptions have been made:

1. The plan writer has relevant executive backing to complete the work.
2. The plan writer has received some training and understands the basic principles of Business Continuity.
3. The organisation has a BC strategy and set objectives.
4. The organisation has a BC Policy that includes purpose and scope.

Summary
Working through this guide will produce the information required to construct a BC Plan which, remember, must be validated with an exercise or activation before it can be considered relevant.

Business Impact Analysis (BIA)

The BIA is the key tool that will provide the information required to build a Business Continuity plan. It will provide a detailed understanding of how the business works, what its key activities are, principal suppliers, people and equipment.

How to start your BIA.

Activities Ask everyone in your team to compile a list of activities that your unit or department carry out on a day to day basis. This list should also include any activity that you are compelled to do by legislation or regulators. After removing duplicates activities, put all the lists together to produce a master list.

Do not worry if the list becomes lengthy, the next part of the process will reduce it considerably.

Activities for Unit or Department

1. ..
2. ..
3. ..
4. ..
5. ..
6. ..

Impact of Loss over Time. In order to establish which of your activities is "(time critical)", the impact of their loss over time must be risk assessed. To do this, use the form below, and set the impact, as **minimal, noticeable, major** or **disaster** against each activity and period.

The period of time that you use is a judgement you must make based on the kind of activity. So, if none of your activities are impacted after an hour of loss, then do not use that category, change it to one which is more relevant. **NB.** Whilst the list illustrated deals with operational impact, reputation and financial impact can also be considered, at the same time or later.

Activity 1...........Impact after 1 hr–minimal.
             Impact after 1 day-minimal
             Impact after 3 days-**major**

Activity 2.........Impact after 1 hr–noticeable
             Impact after 1 day-**major**
             Impact after 3 days-disaster

Activity 3.,......Impact after 1 hr–**major**
             Impact after 1 da -disaster
             Impact after 3 days- disaster

Activity 4.........Impact after 1 hr–minimal.
             Impact after 1 day- minimal
             Impact after 3 days–minimal
             Impact after 1 wk.-minimal

As can be seen from the example above, the impact assessment will highlight those activities that are "time critical" to the organisation, and so will produce a priority list. In this case the impact of stopping activity 4 for a week is minimal, whereas activity 3 is major after 1 hr, activity 2 is major after a day, and activity 1 is major after three days. The "time critical" activities that this element identifies are essential to the continuation of key business services, so will need mitigation where possible and a Business Continuity plan. Some organisations feel that if the risk has been mitigated sufficiently, not all critical activities will need a plan. Personally, I think that if an activity is a critical one, then it should have a plan attached to it.

There will be some units whose disruption of activities may not impact the business for a week or more, but then become critical very quickly. A good example of this is the business pay run, which only becomes critical at certain times of the month. In these cases, the plan should identify when action on these particular activities should be taken.

There will also be some units whose disruption of activities may not impact the business for two weeks or more. This is not a bad thing, because these units can be called upon to assist those who are facing difficulty. If you have units like this, it is worth mapping out the skills within that area of business, so you understand where they can assist.

Time Critical Activities. Now that a list of "time critical" activities has been generated, identify a minimum level of service / Minimum Business Continuity objective (MBCO) to be delivered for each one.

The minimum level of service is by definition less than day to day business but ensures that the time critical activity is maintained. The Recovery Time Objective (RTO) is the time within which at least the minimum level of service will be resumed after a disruption.

Activity 1. E.g. Collect city residents recycling, garden and landfill dustbins once fortnightly. Required 16x staff 8x collection vehicles.

Activity 1. Recovery Time objective (RTO) – 24hrs.

Activity 1. Minimum Level of Service / MBCO - Collect landfill dustbins only, once fortnightly. Required 8x staff 4x Collection vehicles.

Resources. For each of the time critical activities set out the resources required to carry it out at normal levels of service, plus those resources required to carry out the minimum level of service after disruption.

Resources should include – Key staff, skills, building, equipment, vehicles, software, IT systems, specialist equipment and outside suppliers. This is not an exhaustive list, you may find some activities have quite unique needs.

NB -: A common mistake when collecting this information is to add up all of the key staff for each activity and set that as a minimum, when in fact the same staff may carry out a number of activities.

Single Points of Failure. The BIA is likely to uncover unacceptable concentrations of risk, known as single points of failure. These can occur in the most unlikely of places, but most usually consists of key information or skills that reside in a single member of the team. This can easily be remedied by some additional training, or simply recording the knowledge in the BC plan, but can cause severe disruption if not dealt with.

Risk Assessment / Risk Reduction. Now that the time critical activities have been established, consider the risks to their delivery. The risks set out below are the most common, but in some specialist roles, there may be others. Assess the impact on the activity against each risk to delivery, and mitigate where possible.

For instance, if the activity requires a building, or a specialist building, then a fallback position should be developed as a risk control measure. Note that other areas of the organisation may be responsible for maintaining some of the services that you need in order to carry out your activities, so not all of the risk reduction will be for you to develop.

- The common risks to delivery of activities are:
- Loss of access to main building
- ICT systems, telephony
- Data, power
- Water, Fuel
- Supplies
- Reduction in staff.

As I have already said, there may be others that are unique to a particular activity that you will have to plan for.

When this information has been gathered, then a Business Continuity Plan can be developed from it, focussing on the solutions for the remaining risks. Use the Plan template in Appendix D of the BC Policy to produce your plan.

Policy Template Appendix D – Business Continuity Plan

Add company logo here.

Business Continuity Plan for....

Protective Marking: **If Required**

Emergency Response:
Saving life and responding to an emergency comes first. The safety of staff and informing relevant emergency services where appropriate is a prime responsibility and takes precedence over the activation of this plan.

To activate this plan, go to the page indicated for each time critical activity below.

Recovery priorities for Critical Activities: *List department / unit time critical activities in the order you want them recovered.*

1. .	Page
2. .	Page
3. .	Page
4. .	Page
5. .	Page

If you do not want to activate the plan, but wish to become acquainted with the details – see table of contents below:

Table of Contents	Page
Emergency Response	1
Recovery Priorities for this plan	1
When to activate this plan	
Critical Activity 1	
Critical Activity 2	
Critical Activity 3	
Critical Activity 4	
Plan description, scope and purpose	
Risks to delivery, command structure and responsibilities	
Incident management team and room location	
Plan activation	
Recovery Phase	
Annexes	
• **A**. Communications plan	
• **B**. Telephone contact list	
• **C**. Incident Management Team Meeting Suggested Agenda	
• **D**. Additional Task Lists	
• **E**. Evacuation and welfare details	
• **F**. Associated or linked BC plans	
• **G.**	
Document Information	

Activation Criteria - When to Activate this Plan:

Risk to delivery and loss of:	Local Management Arrangements	Plan Escalation Direction	
		1 Contact senior manager, Incident manager, consider BC arrangements	**2** Incident management team, crisis management team, organisation recovery teams formed
Staff	Duty manager or team leader will manage situation.	Large scale loss of staff, unable to maintain business as usual. See BC Plan.	Large loss of staff for more than 2 weeks.
Key Building	Local evacuation procedures will apply.	Loss of critical site for more than 4 hrs likely. Activate fall-back site. See BC Plan.	Loss of key building for more than 2 Weeks.
IT / Data	Help desk or service desk will deal in the first instance.	Loss of critical IT for more than 4hrs. Consider fall back site. See BC Plan.	Loss of key systems for more than 24hrs likely.
Power	Standby generator will activate, restore power.	Loss of generator power for more than 24hrs. Consider fall-back plan. See BC plan.	Loss of main power or generated power for more than 1 week.

Critical Activity 1

Minimum BC Objective: *Using information from your BIA, detail the minimum level of service that this activity will deliver, and the minimum staff required.*

Recovery Time Objective: *Using the information from your BIA, detail what the recovery time objective is for this activity.*

Recovery Procedures: *Detail the recovery procedures, actions and tasks per risk. Also detail the resources required to deliver your minimum level of service recovery. Consider fall-back site, equipment, communications, data management, PPE, records, security, internal / external dependencies / suppliers if any.*

The decision to invoke this Continuity Plan will be a matter of professional judgement; in any case the process must be started in sufficient time to ensure that the objectives are met.

To assist in this decision an activation impact criteria chart has been provided on page 3.

Building Not Available: Fall-back Site Location:
Activate Fall-back Site
1.
2.
Fall-back Resources Information:
1.
2.
Computer Network Fails:
1.
2.
Network Failure Resources Information:

1.

2.

Telephone Network Fails:

1.

2.

Telephone Failure Resources Information:

1.

2.

Staff Shortage:

1.

2.

Staff Shortage Resources Information:

1.

2.

Loss of Key Supplier / Specialist Equipment:

1.

2.

Supplier Resources Information:

1.

2.

Critical Activity 2

Minimum BC Objective: *Using information from your BIA, detail the minimum level of service that this activity will deliver, and the minimum staff required.*

Recovery Time Objective: *Using information from your BIA, detail what the recovery time objective is for this activity.*

Recovery Procedures: *Detail the recovery procedures, actions and tasks per risk. Also, detail the resources required to deliver your minimum level of service recovery. Consider fall-back site, equipment, communications, data management, PPE, records, security, internal / external dependencies / suppliers if any.*

The decision to invoke this Continuity Plan will be a matter of professional judgement; in any case the process must be started in sufficient time to ensure that the objectives are met.

To assist in this decision an activation impact criteria chart has been provided on page 3.

Building Not Available: Fall-back Site Location:
Activate Fall-back Site
1.
2.
Fall-back Resources Information:
1.
2.
Computer Network Fails:
1.
2.
Network Failure Resources Information:
1.
2.
Telephone Network Fails:
1.
2.
Telephone Failure Resources Information:
1.
2.
Staff Shortage:
1.

2.
Staff Shortage Resources Information:
1.
2.
Loss of Key Supplier / Specialist Equipment:
1.
2.
Supplier Resources Information:
1.
2.

Plan Description: This Plan represents *insert department name* Department's arrangements to ensure that it can deliver essential services in line with organisational priorities

Scope: *Detail the scope of the plan.*
This plan assumes that we may be unable to provide Departmental services in the normal way, perhaps through severe staff shortages or loss of primary accommodation. It contains arrangements to provide a minimum level of service, and provisions for alternative working practices and locations that will ensure the time critical activities of the Department can be maintained during a disruption.

To provide a minimum level of service for a protracted period, the following departmental activities will be temporarily suspended: *List the activities in your area of work that will be suspended during a disruption. This list can be obtained from the BIA.*

1.
2.

Purpose: *Detail the purpose of the plan.*
This plan describes the methods by which the *department name* will maintain our critical activities when faced with an incident that may impact significantly on delivery of normal services for a protracted period.

Risks to Delivery: *List the most likely risks to delivery, this list can change according to the type of activity being delivered.*

- Loss of access to main buildings
- Substantial reduction in staff, key personnel
- Loss of IT systems, telecommunications, data, information
- Loss of electrical power, water supply, fuel
- Loss of key supplier / specialist equipment

Command Structure and Responsibilities: The structure below sets out the format that will be used to command all *name of department* BC disruptions.

"You may feel that the Gold, Silver Bronze structure is too formalised for your departmental BC plan command and will confuse other staff used to this structure in larger incidents. If that is the case, you should change the template to suit your needs."

**Incident Management Team for ....
Department:** *Insert the names of the staff in your department that will take on the roles of Gold, Silver and Bronze.*

Incident Management Room / Location: *Identify a location or locations where the incident will be managed from. This will be the focal point for all activity during the disruption. Depending on the size of your organisation, a second alternative may be worthwhile.*

Gold: (insert name) Head of *departments name* has overall strategic responsibility for the Business Continuity response and recovery phases. Suggested Task List in Annex D.

Silver: (role title) are the senior management team for *departments name* and are responsible for the tactics for delivery of departmental critical activities, management of the ongoing recovery process and communications with Gold. Suggested Task List in Annex D.

Bronze/s: (insert name/s) will form the Bronze team/s that will recover the critical activity that has been lost and manage the delivery of a minimum level of service to its pre-determined level. Suggested Task List in Annex D.

Plan Activation: *Who can activate the plan, when and how? Change the text below to suit your own plan.*
This plan, or any part of it, may be invoked either by Organisation Gold or any of *departments name* senior management team in circumstances where they believe that it is not possible to continue to deliver these functions in the normal way and the consequences are such that it may have significant implications for the delivery of normal operations for a protracted period.

The decision to invoke this Continuity Plan will be a matter of professional judgement; in any case the process must be started in sufficient time to ensure that the recovery priorities are met.

To assist in this decision-making process, a plan activation chart has been provided on page 3.

The person invoking the Continuity Plan should consider:

- Consider immediate staff welfare requirements / evacuation if appropriate
- If out-of-hours, consider activating the communications plan Annex A
- Assess the extent of the disruption and confirm the need to invoke this plan using the Activation Criteria chart on page 3.
- Commence incident / decision log.
- Refer to the most relevant recovery plan for the situation encountered
- Call out the relevant Duty Manager – use appropriate call out system for org.
- Consider informing Organisation Gold Commander.
- Consider contacting organisation Media relations staff
- Retain Command and Control until the arrival of the Senior Manager
- Consider appointing supervisors / team leaders for bronze functions e.g. key skills and logistics

The Head of *departments name* **or their Deputy, once informed, will be responsible for continuity arrangements. They will:**

- Assume the role of Gold (Continuity), except in circumstances where there is, or is potential for, organisation - wide impact, in which case management of the incident will be the responsibility of organisation Gold or Executive Officer. In these circumstances, they will assume the role of Silver.
- Gather information, assess the extent of the disruption and confirm the need to invoke this plan.
- Open a decision / Policy log
- If the disruption is wide-ranging, liaise with organisation Gold, asses the need to invoke any other relevant or related plans.

Recovery Phase: When the immediate effects of the incident have been overcome, execute detailed site evaluation, if required. Depending on the size and nature of the disruption, recovery can be complex and may involve more agencies than were used in the response phase e.g. facilities, estates, IT dept.

After a major disruption consider the following actions:

- Ensure a strategy is in place to inform any displaced staff of new working arrangements and to support staff welfare.
- Determine period for which buildings (or part of) may be uninhabitable. Obtain a professional assessment where appropriate
- Determine any temporary arrangements / accommodation to assist the recovery phase

- Identify and provide for any special security arrangements resulting from personnel relocation
- Reassess the recovery plan on a regular basis
- Develop and implement a stand-down plan at the appropriate time to ensure a smooth transition to normality.

A localised disruption may be less impactive and so recovered more easily using departmental structures and resources.

Standing down: Standing down from a Business Continuity Incident will be at the discretion of the Organisation Level Recovery Team or the Head of the affected department / Duty Manager if the incident is more localised.

Annex A
Internal Communications Plan

There are any number of reasons that could result in staff working from home or another location within the organisation area. The most likely causes are Influenza, Norovirus, severe weather, or usual place of work not available.

This plan has been set up to maintain communications with staff working under those conditions, when we cannot communicate with them in the usual way.

It is important to have an uncomplicated way of communicating with staff during a disruption or when dispersed that is accessible to all. The following suggestions are not the only way this can be done but is designed to give you some ideas that might suit you and the way your team works.

Right People, Right Place, Right Time

- *A simple list of all the teams contact numbers kept by managers / team leaders – personal numbers should not be published within the plan.*
- *A snapshot of organisation phone list may be able to be downloaded onto managers work mobiles.*
- *Depending on organisations arrangements with Microsoft, you may be able to use "Outlook" to send your team a group text message. You may already have a bulk messaging system that can be utilised.*
- *Make a page of your outward facing website accessible to staff, where you can publish advice and guidance during a disruption.*
- *Set up a Public Sector BT Meetme account that will allow managers to contact staff via a conference call. The set-up cost is free to the Public Sector, but there is a cost for calls.*
- *Prior to any disruption, and you have office 365, set up a group within Microsoft Lync that can be used to message the team as a group. Also, if the team are dispersed and using laptops, Lync can be used for video conferencing.*

The internal communications plan can be activated under these conditions:

- If for any reason a disruption is expected, then staff can be warned in advance that they will be working elsewhere, and the communications plan will be activated on a given date.
- In the event of an unexpected disruption, such as a power failure or fire, the duty manager / team leader will inform staff using the preferred communications method in this plan.

Plan Execution (This is a suggested format. Change it as you see fit or delete entirely.)

- 0800 – Senior Management team (SMT) / Duty Manager conduct conference call to discuss: a. department strategy during the disruption, b. Staff Issues, c. Incidents, d. Department messages, e. Other subjects as required.
- 0830- All Managers / Team Leaders to call in on the conference call for a briefing from SMT or their representative.
- 0900 – Managers / team leaders host conference call with staff that are working from home or alternative locations and communicate messages from 0800 meeting. All other staff will be informed using usual methods of communication if they are available.
- 1530 – Managers / Team Leaders host conference call with staff that are working from home or alternative locations, pick up staff issues, incidents arising during the day.
- 1600 – Senior Management Team / Duty Manager conduct conference call to pick up on issues fed back by staff to managers / team leaders and set agenda / actions for following day's 0800 conference.

Annex B
Telephone Contact List
Name.   Role.   Contact   No.

Annex C
Incident Management Team

The suggestions for these agenda items are based on the JESIP joint decision model, which is a tried and tested way of approaching decisions. Printed by kind permission of the Joint Emergency Services programme.

Suggested Agenda

Gather information and intelligence
- Introductions (roles/responsibilities) - Identify individual to record actions
- Any items requiring urgent attention - Take action where needed
- Situation report – reason for plan activation -
- Update from all departments -

Assess risks and develop a working strategy
- Assess impact on staff and review welfare / health and safety
- Assess likely recovery time - Prioritise recovery of services if required
- Assess impact on critical services - List critical activities affected
- Assess impact on related activities - There will be some services interrelated with critical activities.
- Develop or review initial working strategy – If a large disruption, refer to organisation strategy.

Consider powers, policies and procedures
- If organisation wide – agree areas of responsibility with crisis team
- Consider areas of responsibility – appoint bronzes as required.

- Identify relevant policies, legislation and procedures – Finance, Estates, HR.

Identify options and contingencies

- Review current actions on recovery of critical activities – may need to be prioritised
- Consider if additional actions are required to prevent further loss of service.
- Consider options based on circumstances and not covered in the BC Plan.
- Consider additional contingencies should disruption escalate – identify and prepare.
- Consider internal and external communications messages to staff and interested parties.
- Are the right people at this meeting – who else should attend?
- Consider mutual aid from other departments / organisations / voluntary sector / partners.
- Are all actions and decisions supported by the company ethos, ethics and codes of practice?
- Any other business – Time and location of next meeting

Take action and review what happened

- Close meeting – Implement actions
- If organisation wide – give update to organisation crisis team
- Ensure update on actions is available for next meeting.

Annex D   Additional Task Lists

This annex can be used to contain any additional task lists that you may feel are relevant to your plan that will assist or guide those who have tasks within it. If there are none, then delete.

Annex E   Evacuation and Welfare Details

This annex can be used to contain any evacuation and welfare arrangements that have been made for staff in the event of a disruption. It may also contain details of any specific arrangements for staff who have existing disabilities, temporary disabilities, or other issues that require reasonable adjustments to be made.

Annex F   Associated Business Continuity Plans

This annex can be used to contain the details of any existing Business Continuity plans that are linked or associated to this one and may be of use during a disruption.

Document Information
Document Name

Document approval: *The document should be approved by Chief Executive, Head of department or unit manager.*

Approved by:

Date:

Version Control.

Version number:

Date:

Author:

Authorised by/Approval

Distribution:

Update History.

Version: Person Updating: Date:

Revision Description:

Version: Person Updating: Date:
Revision Description:

Version: Person Updating: Date:
Revision Description:

Last Exercise or Activation.
Date:
Activation type :
Comments:

Date:
Activation type – Exercise or Live:
Comments:

Documents to Support this Plan:
Document name:
Where stored:

Document name:
Where stored:

Annual Review:
Reviewer Name:
Date

Template 2: Terms of Reference for BC Group Meeting

Principal Aims

- To promote a co-ordinated, and where appropriate, common approach to Business Continuity Management through shared working practices relating to strategy, Policy, procedure, resources, training, exercising and plan development across the whole organisation.
- To maintain links with our Business Continuity Representatives.
- To exchange best practice and lessons learned through plan development, activations and disruptions.
- To provide a formalised structure, within which risks identified by the Business Continuity process and not dealt with locally, can be escalated to the relevant executive board for decision.
- To provide a formalised structure for the dissemination of Business Continuity actions as directed by the relevant executive board.

Membership

- Organisation Business Continuity Representatives, not role specific.
- Organisation Risk Manager.

Meetings

Meetings will be held quarterly at *state meeting place.*

Depending on circumstances, guests with expertise in specific areas may be invited to give presentations to the group.

- Minutes and actions will be circulated as soon as possible after the meeting and in any case no later than two weeks.
- Papers for the meeting will be circulated at least one week prior to the meeting date.

Office Holders

The meetings will be chaired by the Business Continuity Coordinator / Manager, who will make arrangements for minute taking.

Standard Agenda

1. Apologies   Chair
2. Minutes of last meeting   Chair
3. Update on actions from previous meetings   All
4. Update from regional group. Nominated Representative
5. Update from relevant executive board.   Nominated Representative
6. Incidents / Plan activations   All
7. BC Exercise All
8. New / emerging requirements, standards and / or practices All
9. Training Chair
10. Any other business   All
11. Date of next meeting and venue All

12 SAMPLE EXERCISE SCENARIOS

Exercise Scenario 1 - Severe Weather
Aim
To review the BC arrangements for severe weather

Objectives
- To review the arrangements in individual BC plans for severe weather
- To review the arrangements in individual BC plans for loss of patrol vehicles
- To review the communications arrangements with staff in BC plans

Scenario
Any week day
The Met Office forecast that there will be a snow fall in the next 24hrs which is likely to cause some minor traffic problems.

Inject 1
The Met Office have updated their forecast, and increase their level of confidence to very high, that there will be a significant snowfall causing major disruption to roads across the county and have issued an Amber warning for snow.

Question -

1. Does your BC Plan advise any actions at this point, if so what are they?

Facilitator expectations. Plans may advise initial actions on, staff disruption, 4x4 vehicles, media messages.

2. What does your plan say about communicating with staff under these circumstances?

Facilitator expectations. Looking to see some pre-emptive messages concerning snow, advice from force weather pages, communications with disrupted staff.

Inject 2

The Met Office forecast is accurate and overnight 6" of snow falls, disrupting all major routes. A severe weather group is formed with an organisation Gold appointed. The snow is likely to persist for over 1 week. The organisation has advised staff that if it is too hazardous to travel, then they should attend their nearest place of work, or work remotely.

Question -

1. What are your critical activities at this point?

Facilitator expectations. Plan should outline what the critical activities are and the minimum level of service that is to be delivered.

2. What skill level of staff do you expect to attend your building?

Facilitator expectations. This should reflect experience from the past, skill levels of other staff attending that don't usually work at that location.

Summary notes

If snow is not a regular disruption for your area, plans may not reflect a response. Essentially snow is a denial of a building, so any snow actions could easily be an annex to the loss of building plan.

Exercise Scenario 2 - Loss of Staff
Aim
To review the BC arrangements for a reduction of staff

Objectives
- To review the arrangements in individual BC plans for a reduction in staff
- To identify activation criteria for reduction in staff
- To identify any single points of failure when key staff are absent

Scenario
9am any week day
Several staff have reported sick with norovirus (winter vomiting disease).
Inject 1
This is highly contagious, and it is likely in the next 48 to 72 hrs an increasing number of staff will be absent.

Question -
1. What percentage / number of staff absence will cause you to activate your BC plan?

Facilitator expectations. All plans should have activation criteria that indicate the levels of staff that are required, and an escalation process as to when to activate the plan and who to inform. In small team's plan activation will occur more quickly.

2. Do any of your critical activities rely on the unique skills of a single person, if so how is this managed when they are absent?

Facilitator expectations. All single points of failure should be understood; however, the exercise may highlight additional areas that require attention. Skills need not be perfectly matched but should be sufficient to deliver the minimum level of service.

Inject 2

Because of staff reluctance to report sick, they have come into work still infectious, as a consequence the infection and absence rate has reached 70% across your department. This is set to persist for the next week.

Question -

1. What instruction / advice does your BC plan contain about this level of staff absence?

Longer shifts, cancellation of leave and time off may be an option at this point, assistance from other departments.

2. Will this level of absence have an effect on your critical activities and minimum level of service, if so what?

Facilitator expectations. Minimum levels of service may well be affected at this point. Critical activities may need to be re prioritised in the light of this situation, unless key staff can be found. A good indicator of minimum staffing would be those levels used during school holidays in August and between January and March when staff use up leave before April. The organisation sustains all its activities and performance during this time.

Summary notes
Staff shortages can be created by a number of events, pandemic, large mobilisation, and severe weather. It is important that minimum staffing levels are realistic, and plans articulate what level of service they can deliver, what the escalation process is, any single point of failure, and work around that may be necessary.

Learning
Note what lessons have been identified in this exercise, and what changes if any have been made to your plans.

Exercise Scenario 3 - Loss of Building

Aim
To review the BC arrangements for the loss of a key building

Objectives
- To review the arrangements in individual BC plans for this loss
- To identify activation criteria for fallback location
- To identify communications process if fallback location activated

Scenario
10am week day

Whilst replacing a ceiling in your building, workmen have disturbed a significant quantity of asbestos. Because this poses a health hazard, the building has been evacuated with staff currently congregated at evacuation muster points.

Inject 1
Whilst at the muster points, you are advised that it will be at least 24hrs before the building can be re occupied.

Question -

1. Does your building have an evacuation plan, if so is it referenced in your BC plan?

The BC plan should reference the evacuation plan along with the muster point information.

2. What does your BC plan say about activating your fallback site and staff welfare?

Facilitator expectations. The plan should detail all that is needed to leave the current building and go to the fallback site. Communications with staff, welfare, travel and continued attendance should also be covered.

Inject 2

It will be at least two weeks before the building can be made safe for reoccupation.

Question -

1. What if any will be the impact of your additional staff on the fallback site?

Are there sufficient resources available, can the infrastructure cope, will it house everyone, or will some be sent home or elsewhere?

2. What is the maximum period you can occupy your fallback site?

3. What other issues would arise from a prolonged occupation of the fallback site?

Facilitator expectations. Staff association issues, travelling costs, additional stress of working in an unfamiliar environment, longer shift patterns, welfare issues.

Summary notes

The loss of a building or part of a building for whatever reason is a realistic prospect, with a high impact. Plans should contain reliable options for this contingency. In 2015 part of the main Police station in Southampton was unavailable for this reason.

Lessons identified

What lessons have been identified from this exercise?

Exercise Scenario 4 - ICT Failure

Aim
To review organisation BC arrangements for loss of ICT Network

Objectives
- To review the arrangements in individual BC plans for this loss
- To identify local command and control process for widespread ICT network failure
- To identify the communications process if there was IT network failure

Scenario
Your department has over (add number) employees, and is responsible for the following critical functions:
- Add core business activity
- Add core business activity
- Add core business activity
- Add core business activity

Inject 1
0700 Any week day

Senior managers have been informed by ICT that a "denial of service attack" on our organisation by the group "Anonymous Hackers" has caused our network to fail. Therefore, all the organisations computers will not be able to log in to the network for the next two hours whilst the problem is assessed. Those areas of business that have voice over internet protocol telephony may not be able to receive calls for this period.

Question –

1. What local arrangements if any will be enacted to manage the disruption and maintain critical services on your department or service?

Facilitator expectations. Airwave not affected, expect divisions to be able to carry on response as normal. All the network telephones will not work. The remaining analogue telephony will work as normal. Will expect to see what critical services will be affected, and whether there are paperwork systems in place for those that are.

2. How will staff and suppliers be communicated with?

Facilitator expectations. Possible use of organisation text service to inform staff. Possible use of internet page, as for severe weather. Mobiles for contact of suppliers, would expect to see suppliers phone details in the plan.

3. What local command and control process would be enacted, if any, to manage the BC issues?

Facilitator expectations. This is an organisation wide issue so Gold group would run. Senior manager would set up local group. Management and control of paperwork systems for those areas that required it. Some groups may not be affected at all.

Inject 2

Two hours later

The head of ICT has informed the organisation that the network services will not be available for the next 24hrs to allow the network switches to be re booted, after which it will be gradually restored.

Question -

1. What additional problems does this now create?

Facilitator expectations. This is likely to cause a large backlog of paper information that will need inputting once systems return. Arrangements for additional staff to do the input should be considered during the recovery. Where do we keep the resulting paper after input, could it be required for disclosure? Loss of intelligence from existing systems, loss of new intel, loss of niche, mobile data, web storm and much more. Safety of officers attending calls without up to date intel

Summary notes.

The likelihood of this scenario is low, but the impact is very high. The computer network is a highly resilient system that can reroute automatically when is senses a problem. So, what is more likely, is that parts of the network could fail, producing the same effect but in isolated pockets, rather than force wide. Cyber-attack is in the top 5 of national risks identified.

Having paperwork alternatives for important processes is crucial, as there are any number of things that can cause a key system to fail.

Learning

What lessons have been identified in this exercise?

Exercise Scenario 5 – Loss of Power

Aim
To establish how effective BC plans are against a loss of power.

Objectives

- Identify which time critical/prioritised activity would be affected and for how long during a power failure.
- How effective is the planned response that is contained within current BC Plans?

Inject 1
Road works have dug up a cable that has caused a local electricity substation to fail, causing a total loss of power to your main building. It is 11am on a Monday morning in November and the temperature is falling. The heating is off, and the electricity provider has said that they hope to restore power by 1.30pm.

Question.

1. What impact if any does this have on your time critical activities
2. Who will be affected by the outage
3. What is your plan for the rest of the day
4. What does your BC plan say about this?

Inject 2
The electricity company now say that it will be 72 hours before power can be restored.

Question

1. What are the impacts on your time critical activities and the staff working for you.
2. If you have a standby generator how long can it run before needing refuelling.
3. Whose responsibility is it to refuel the generator.
4. What communications processes would you set up to deal with the next 72 hours.
5. What are your priorities.
6. When the power is restored, how long and what preparations will you have to make to return to normal.

Learning

What lessons have been identified in this exercise?

Exercise Scenario 6 – Infectious Disease

Aim
To establish how effective BC plans might be against infectious disease.

Objectives
- Explore how BC Plans might be used as a capability
- How effective is the planned response that is contained within current BC Plans?

Information
Norovirus, sometimes known as the winter vomiting bug in the UK is the most common cause of viral gastroenteritis in humans. Transmitted fecally by contaminated food or water, by person to person contact, and via aerosolisation of vomited virus and contaminated surfaces.
The unpleasant effects usually last for two to three days.
Often been the ruin of many a cruise.

Inject 1
The time is 0750 on a Wednesday in your canteen.
You hear in the coffee queue that a member of staff in the canteen has reported sick with the virus. No other cases have been reported.

Question.
1. Having collected your coffee, what if any, are your considerations at this point regarding your team or department.
2. What actions if any would you take?

Inject 2
The time is 0830 the same day.

You do a bit of research on the subject to find that outbreaks of the virus on cruises and in closed communities have been traced to a single infected person handling food. Currently no cases or impact on your department.

Question

1. Considering the source of the virus, what are the likely outcomes and impact from an outbreak of this kind on your organisation?
2. Escalation, does anyone need to know at this point?
3. Consider infection control measures, what are they?
4. Could your BC Plan assist at this point, consider how you might use it to protect staff against infection.

Inject 3

The time is 10am the same day.

You decide to convene an Incident Management team, who in the first instance decide to send your team to their fallback positions for 1 week.

Question

1. How would you achieve that using your current BC Plan?
2. How would you alert staff members of the plan that are not yet at work?
3. How will you communicate with staff during the week the fallback site or sites is activated?

Inject 4

Your organisation is now running a Gold group on this issue, as at least 10 staff have reported sick. The Gold group have asked the Incident Management Team to make large scale evacuation of your entire department to reduce infection in key staff.

Questions

Can your BC Plan provide the following information for the IMT?

1. A list of fallback locations and the names of personnel who will attend.
2. A list of those who will be working from home.
3. A list of additional skills that are available from staff not engaged in a time critical activity.
4. How you will communicate with them daily.

Learning

What lessons have been identified in this exercise?

143

Made in the USA
Lexington, KY
29 March 2018